AF429341

Amazing Joy

Amazing Joy

Choosing Joy Through All of Life's Journeys

By Melissa Kelly

Amazing Joy

ISBN: 979-8-218-11415-2

Cover image by Melissa Kelly

The names of some individuals featured throughout this book have been changed to protect their privacy.

This book is dedicated to my mom. Her life taught me how to love. Her death taught me how to live. She is my inspiration for this journey of living life to the fullest and never waiting for "tomorrow."

"I'll look back on this and smile because it was life, and I decided to live it." –Anonymous

INTRODUCTION

As I watched the sunrise from the corner table at the donut shop that Friday morning, I contemplated my next move. I stared down at the middle of the glazed donut on my plate and felt like my life had the same hole in the middle of it. I knew something had to change. I was questioning my beliefs, and my friend sitting across from me recognized it too. She knew I had lost my ability to see the joy in life.

Merriam-Webster defines joy as "a state of happiness" and "the emotion evoked by well-being, success or good fortune, or by the prospect of possessing what one desires." According to the definition, it seems as though joy is a result of our circumstances when it's really a choice we make for ourselves each day.

When bad things happen, our natural response is to feel the negative impact of it because that's the easy thing to do. But choosing to respond with joy makes life much more gratifying.

Joy was all around me as a child. It was in the activities I did, in the family that surrounded me, and in the traditions that were being formed. I didn't have to CHOOSE it because the pressures of adulthood weren't there to overpower it. I got to wake up each day and do the things I loved. If it was summer, I got to sleep in, maybe have a playdate with friends and ride bikes, and then have a softball game at the end of the day before staying up late and doing it all again the next day. If it was during the school year, I still woke up looking forward to the day, probably because I got to see my friends at school and then came home to the things I enjoyed. Except for homework, I'm not sure I ever enjoyed that.

What happens when our childlike joy begins to fade? Will we let the demands of adulthood steal our happiness? Or will we wake up every day and fight to choose joy? Choosing joy is not easy. It takes work. With the help of a great counselor, I was able to put in the work and climb out of the dark days, which were a result of grief and depression and being mad that my life didn't turn out like I thought it would. The effort it takes to choose joy every day is worth it to me because I'm a much better version of myself when I'm choosing joy.

This is the story of my personal journey when I realized I wanted more out of life and decided to wake up each day and choose joy.

CHAPTER 1

My journey began many years ago in Missouri. I was born and raised in a one-stoplight town full of farming and football, where we heard the train whistle blow multiple times an hour.

We lived in a 3-bedroom house built by my dad and others the year I was born, with every room having a different color of carpet. I eventually gave up trying to match the décor in my room to the lovely green shag carpet I walked on each time I stepped through the doorway. The values instilled in me that I've carried throughout my lifetime began in that house. Values like the importance of family, Christian beliefs, managing finances, and weekly chores. Ok, maybe only some of those stuck with me because I sure don't dust every weekend like I was instructed to do every Saturday morning as a kid.

It wasn't just a house to me, though. It was my home for the next 22 years and made me feel as secure as our basement did anytime a tornado rolled through town. The same basement where my mom kept all the canned goods from the garden and where we often played as kids. Especially when the air hockey table arrived, it became a great hangout spot for our friends.

My first memories of music are the tunes that blared from the living room record player as my parents played cards on Saturday night with friends. The sounds of Neil Diamond and Cat Stevens still ring in my head. And today, that same record player now sits in my office. As soon as I put on Cat Stevens' *Tea For The Tillerman*, I'm immediately taken back to the smell of cheese dip and the sounds of laughter coming from the kitchen.

Our Sunday night dinners were reserved for popcorn, made the old-fashioned way on the stove. The secret ingredient? Bacon grease in place of oil to coat the kernels. So, if you were ever at our house and wondered why there was a jar in the refrigerator labeled "bacon grease," now you know what it was for! And our favorite side to accompany the popcorn, although usually only made on special occasions, was Grandma's Popcorn Fudge. It's not your typical soft, chewy fudge, but when cooked just right, it's broken into pieces and has just a smidge of crispness.

The lifelong values I was taught beginning at a young age were one of the many blessings from my parents, who raised me in the same small town where they grew up. Growing up in the same small town wasn't the only thing they had in common, though. They were both from families who had double-digit offspring.

It still amazes me that two of the largest families in town were united when my parents got married, which resulted in my sister and I being the only two people with bloodlines from both families. I feel honored to be able to say that. I had hoped to carry on that legacy through children of my own, but instead, I will carry on the legacy by helping to keep the memories alive.

As a child, I loved being daddy's little girl. I was typically outside with him whenever he was working in the yard. I rode on his lap while he mowed until I was old enough for him to teach me to ride the mower. And I could often be found at the city's fire station since my dad was a volunteer fireman and Fire Chief for many years.

"I'm leaving for the fire station," he would tell my mom.

But before he could leave, I would stop him and ask, "Can I go too?"

"Sure, hop in the truck," he would tell me just before I darted out the door and ran across the driveway to climb in his little white truck with my ponytail swinging from side to side.

Being near the firetrucks and even getting to ride in them was not the highlight of the trip, though. It was getting to hang out with my dad. It took me a long time to realize he didn't HAVE to take me. But he did. He could have very easily left me at home instead of letting me tag along.

I remember walking in the bay doors and seeing their gear lined up on the wall with their jackets hanging up and boots and pants on the floor to make it easy and quick to put on. But when my dad was the Fire Chief, he would carry his gear in the car so that he could arrive at the fires quickly if he had been at work. His gear wore the smells of house fires and grass fires, and we always knew when he walked into the house after fighting a fire because his clothes also reeked of smoke. It wasn't pleasant, but I was proud knowing he was helping save someone's home.

Fishing and golfing weren't lasting hobbies of my dad's, but I do remember casting a rod and swinging a club with him a few times. I especially love reminiscing about the time he got a speeding ticket while I was in the car with him, and he was afraid my mom would find out. Which is why he paid me $20 to keep it between him and me. I kept my side of the deal and learned that was a good bargaining tip for the future. Sometimes I would just walk up and hold my hand out, and out came his wallet. And then we would laugh about the silly things, which continued to be a joke for years to come.

When it was just him and I spending time together, I looked up to him as he taught me lasting life lessons like respecting others, shaking hands when meeting someone, and leaving big tips. Seeing how he interacted with others made me admire him even more.

Spending time with my dad evolved from yard work to learning how to back a trailer and even learning to be a pyrotechnician. I eagerly gravitated towards the garage whenever he became a fireworks guru. I waited in anticipation for my chance to sit beside him and listened intently as he taught me how to make new beauties in the sky. With his brothers and nephew alongside him, they learned how to create a fireworks display that the entire city looked forward to each year. And on the deck of my parent's house is where we came up with the idea of inventing a candle that smelled like fireworks. We even tried to bottle the smell by capturing the smoke from one of the fuses. The scent lasted as long as the smoke did, which was mere seconds. But hey, we were just kids, so we thought it would be a fun experiment. And when I say kids, I mean we were in our 30s.

Even though I loved being outside with my dad, I also treasured my time inside with my mom. We bonded over puzzles, baking, cross-stitching, and our favorite tv shows like *All My Children*, *Wheel of Fortune*, and the Olympics. But if it was Saturday morning, you would find me watching *Saved By The Bell*…without her. A few of my favorite things to bake with her were her legendary sugar cookies, apple rolls, Chex mix (or party mix as we called it), caramel brownies, and Christmas candy in the plastic molds with the red and green peppermint sprinkles to make the green chocolate glimmer with goodness. She knew all our personal favorites and would make sure I had peanut butter balls to last for days, toffee for my sister, rice crispy clusters for my dad, and turtles which we all fought over. I refused to learn how to cook but would look forward to the moments when we would bake one of her yummy treats together.

I learned how to bake cookies with the perfect doneness, tricks for spreading the caramel between the brownie layers, and how to properly ice a layer cake by first cutting it in half with dental floss. Note, this is one of those times when you probably don't want to use the minty green floss in the cabinet!

With the floss in hand, and the 9x13 cake still on the cooling rack, she would tell me, "Put the floss at the corner of the cake and slowly wiggle it through the center. Once you've reached the other end, you will have two evenly sliced halves."

The smell of the cookies baking in the oven wasn't the only thing radiating throughout the house. My mom's love for me was felt constantly and found in the little things like handwritten notes, my favorite candy in my Easter basket, and packing my school lunch every morning.

Being my mother was one of the many things she did. She was also a homeroom mom, a PTO mom, a Girl Scout leader, a second mom to my friends, and a stay-at-home mom raising my sister and me. The school bus didn't go by our house, so I was the lucky kid who got dropped off and picked up at school. Well, except for kindergarten through 5th grade, when I had to walk to school. Up and down THE HILL. THE GIGANTIC HILL. But I'm not bitter about having to walk up THE STEEP HILL that we had to lean into while walking in order to avoid falling and rolling to the bottom. I'm only exaggerating a little about the size of the hill. Or am I?

When I got home from school every afternoon, Mom always had a snack waiting for me. Cherry Kool-Aid in a glass (which probably came from a McDonald's happy meal) and Funyuns in a plastic cereal bowl were on the counter when I walked in the door. And then, at 5:30 on the dot, dinner would be ready and on the table. To this day, I have no idea how she made sure everything got done at the same time and right as my dad walked in the door after a long day at work. She was a woman of many talents.

Her cooking and baking skills were superb, she had a green thumb and had many beautiful plants inside the house and in her garden, and she could sew anything. Including all the matching clothes she made my sister and me wear as children. She would dress us in one blue and one pink jumpsuit with white blouses underneath to look similar but not like twins. Matching Easter dresses. And the "bubble suit" that was black with pink flowers when we were teenagers. Matching bubble suits along with bangs standing straight up are the memories I cherish, but the pictures I hope nobody ever sees.

I'm thankful for the things she taught me but more thankful for the things I inherited from her. Like her joy for life and her love for her family. She would do anything for her family. She had a smile that lit up a room and a laugh that would turn into a snort. And she had beautiful gray hair that I also inherited at a young age. Thanks, Mom. But you could have kept that one to yourself.

Other than when I was acting like a typical bratty teenager, my relationship with my parents was close. They supported and encouraged me in all my activities, and it always brought a smile to my face when I looked into the stands and saw them cheering me on. They were there every time, whether it was a volleyball game, an awards ceremony, a band concert, a 4th-grade play, or a softball game. My dad frequently went to work early in the mornings just so he could leave in time to attend our activities. The only time he would miss something was when he was putting out fires; as a fireman, he loved being able to help others.

Another lifelong value I learned as a child is the value of a wooden spoon. I can still hear the squeak of the kitchen drawer opening while getting into some mischief with my sister at the other end of the hallway. Our timing was always impeccable too. Wait until Mom is on a phone call and THEN get into a sibling fight. That was poor planning on our part because it usually resulted in a harsher punishment. You'd think we would learn our lesson. We did, however, know to break up the fight as soon as we heard the kitchen drawer start to open. Moms are smarter than that, though, because we still got to feel the sting of the spoon when she caught up with us as we ran through the house to avoid her.

Having a sister three years older than me meant that we were involved in a lot of the same activities. T-ball, Girl Scouts, volleyball, and band, to name a few. And as the younger sister, I got a lot of hand-me-downs. I used to hate getting the leftovers, including the Halloween costumes that my sister had dressed up in before me. The orange bunny costume she wore? Mine the next year. The clown costume? Mine the next year. The princess costume? Yep, mine the next year. Looking back on those things now makes me smile, though. First, I've learned how hard it is to be creative with a new costume each year. And second, I can see my mom's love for us and making sure we had a costume to wear.

As kids, my sister and I played catch in the middle of the dead-end street that we lived on, rode our bikes up and down the hill in front of the house, and played kickball OVER the house as one of us kicked from the front yard, and the other waited in the back for it to fly over. But if the one in the back wasn't quick enough to catch it, the ball would roll down the hill and land in the trees. It was usually retrievable, but only after a hike through the wooded trees and brush.

The street in front of our house sloped just enough to allow for sledding. So, when the winter weather arrived, my sister and I enjoyed getting out the Flexible Flyer wooden sled with the red steel runners and a steerable crossbar at the front. As soon as the snow was packed down enough to use it, or there was ice, we waxed the steel runners and headed outside until our clothes were too wet to continue.

On one particular icy day, while playing outside, my sister said, "Let's sled down the stairs on the side of the house since the snow and ice are high enough to cover them."

"But how will we stop once we reach the backyard and not keep going?" I asked.

That's when she assured me, "I'll stand at the bottom of the stairs and catch you."

I eagerly replied, "Ok, let's do it."

With my plastic sled in hand, I took my place at the top of the stairs, which were dug into the hill on the side of the house. My sister took her place at the bottom, just like she agreed to do. It was much slicker than we anticipated, and at the bottom, where my sister was supposed to catch me, I flew right by her. With the trees in mind, I forgot about the 4-foot ledge at the bottom of the yard, and there wasn't anything to grab onto. I came to a jerking stop right before the drop-off when a metal pole in the garden stopped my descent. It wasn't a pleasant feeling to run into the pole back-first, but I was happy I didn't go over the edge. I WASN'T pleased with my sister, though, who promised to catch me. I tried to climb my way back up to the yard, but my rubber-soled shoes didn't have enough traction to make it. I kept sliding back down. My sister felt bad and offered assistance, but I was mad, and I pouted. For over an hour. Until I finally got cold enough to let her help me.

Even though she didn't catch me that day, my sister still had my back. Except for those times when she was a high school senior and liked picking on her freshman sister. But as the older sister who could drive, she was also nice enough to chauffeur my friends and me around. For softball practice, we would pile seven people in her red 2-door car, and on Saturday nights, she would take a friend and me along to cruise Main Street with her friends. I felt so cool getting to hang out with my older sister and her friends.

I especially like the time we decided to stay up late to "foil" our parent's kitchen in the middle of the night as an April Fool's Day joke. We put foil EVERYWHERE! Covering the cabinets, the stove, and the table, we even wrapped the toaster and mixer in foil like they were Christmas presents. All done while our parents slept at the other end of the house, and somehow never heard the crinkling of the foil as we moved around the kitchen and laughed like two toddlers who were causing mischief. When morning arrived, I pretended to be asleep while eagerly waiting for a reaction from our parents. And to my delight, we heard Mom giggling as she walked into the kitchen. I could barely keep quiet. And then she barreled through my bedroom door, laughing at the cute little prank from her adult children, who happened to be home for the weekend. These are the memories I cherish and the moments I don't want to forget!

Our family of four felt small compared to our extended family. When I was born into two very large families, I wasn't just blessed with a large number on one side. Nope, I got hit with the double whammy of having cousins coming out of the wazoo on both sides of my parent's families. You think I'm kidding? Let me break this down for you. Nineteen biological aunts and uncles and about 60 biological first cousins. SIXTY! And that doesn't include anyone's spouses or my cousins' children. You're crazy if you think I'm going to try counting that number. And in case you're wondering, yes, I can name all of my aunts and uncles in order of birth. Not being able to name all of my second and third cousins becomes interesting at times, though. This is why I have to request an ancestry.com report before dating someone to make sure we're not related!

Growing up in a large family was fun for me. It's all I knew because I had nothing else to compare it to since I had it on both sides. So, when people saw our holidays as crowded, I saw them as comfortable. Nestled into my grandparent's rock house that my grandpa helped build when he was a child, we piled into the living room like sardines in a can. As my generation grew older and began having kids, the family grew, and the house got smaller. We had to squeeze into any available corner to get out of the way of others trying to walk by. Seating was minimal, so the stone ledge in front of the fireplace was a popular place to sit once the couch filled up. I think our family might be the ones that came up with the phrase "place back" because it was yelled so much when someone left the room.

Family traditions are another thing I learned at a young age and they are probably at fault for my being sentimental. Growing up in a stable, always predictable environment created the beginnings of my safety net, which grew larger and larger as the predictability continued. By the time I went to college, I had a safety net large enough to catch a trapeze artist if they fell while flying through the air. I had traditions on both sides of my family, and we almost always knew our holiday plans because they were the same every year. Although, every year, we still had to ask what time lunch started for each holiday. 1:00. It starts at 1:00.

When it came to Easter, Thanksgiving, and Christmas holiday dinners, it wouldn't have been real if we hadn't touched elbows at the table as we ate. We had our routine down to a science, including knowing that we had to eat as we put food on our plates; otherwise, we would run out of room before all the food made it around the table.

But every year, without fail, when we sat down at the table, someone would ask, "Which way are we passing?"

And almost in unison, the rest of the family would say, "To the right."

I was just happy when I got to sit at the adult table. With a family as big as ours, there were only so many available spots at the table, which stretched from the fireplace to the other end of the house.

It was jam-packed on the paternal side of the family too, and again, it felt comfortable to me because it's what we always did. The men would huddle in the kitchen, and whether you were in the back room or outside, you could hear their contagious laughter. Whenever we heard their harmonious roars, we immediately wanted to know the joke or the story. The punchline was hardly ever repeated, but that didn't stop the rest of us from giggling as we watched my dad and uncles hunched over in amusement.

We had different traditions on each side of the family, and thankfully each was celebrated at a different time, so we didn't have to choose which one to attend. But one thing that wasn't different was how my grandparents on both sides made sure that every grandchild got a present for Christmas. This probably sounds obvious for a grandparent to do, but keep in mind they each had about 30 grandchildren to buy for. That's a lot of shopping!

Looking back on our family holidays, it's not the presents that I remember. It's the time we had together, the memories created, and the VHS tapes to relive it. I will never forget the infamous game of Spoons that is still talked about. Are you familiar with the game? It's played with a deck of cards and spoons. Yes, spoons from the utensil drawer. The number of spoons used in the game is one less than the number of players. The goal is to get a four-of-a-kind, and the first person to do it reaches for a spoon. And then it's a race for the others to grab a spoon. The person who doesn't get a spoon is out the next round. Similar to musical chairs.

Anyone who has played Spoons knows that it can get very competitive and sometimes even dangerous. I've been in games where women's fingernails have left scratch marks on other players. But the particular game of Spoons that our family will never forget involved one of my uncles diving for the last spoon in order to stay in the game. The problem is that he dove from one end of the wooden 6-foot table to the other end. And that's when it happened. The top of the table came apart from the base and was now on its side while everyone tried to hold it up. The handmade table that was a precious heirloom to my grandma was now in two pieces. Grandma Rose yelled from the kitchen, "You boys are grounded!" Even though they were adults and didn't live at home anymore. Her face and her reaction are something that none of us wanted to witness that day, and it's something that we will never forget. Because that's the day that we got banned from playing Spoons on her dining room table!

Our holiday traditions and stories that get repeated to each new generation are a sign of the love we have for each other. Family time is where I learned to love others, and family gatherings are one of the things I love most in life.

Even as an adult, you will often find me spending time with my family on the weekends. I have always enjoyed being close to home so that I could spend holidays with family and my vacation weeks hanging out with my mom. I always thought spending time at home was for my benefit, but when I look back now, I think it was for my mom too. It was a cherished time we would never get more of, so I'm thankful for those weekends and holidays. Time is something I always thought we had plenty of. I also thought I would watch my parents grow old together. And even when my mom got sick, I still thought both of these things.

CHAPTER 2

Spending time with family is something I have always enjoyed doing. And one of our favorite ways to spend time together is by traveling.

My experience with road trips started at the early age of six months old. I can remember it vividly… Pikes Peak mountain in the background, our silver car, and me in a car seat on the hood of the car. Oh wait, that's the image from the Polaroid picture inside our family photo album. But I was still six months old, and we still went to Pikes Peak.

Our adventures as a family were a regular occurrence. There were a few out-of-state road trips, but most of the vacations we took when I was young were to a local theme park. I cherish the memories of the Orient Express clicking as the roller coaster cars went up the first hill just in time for us to reach the top and to start speeding to the end as my head bounced back and forth between the shoulder harness. I was tall enough to ride but not tall enough for my head to be above the harness. I quickly learned not to wear earrings on that ride because they would poke me as my head jolted from side to side and pressed against the harness. But that never stopped me from standing in line and doing it again.

I used to hate the drive to the theme park because it seemed long at the time, and it always felt like it took forever to arrive at our destination. But looking back on it now, I have realized the journey was just as big as the destination. We had a lot of fun in the car on our way there by playing slug-bug and the license plate game in between the occasional sibling fights due to one of us crossing the invisible line and ending up on the other's side of the backseat. But that was part of the fun, too, and the memories that were made.

We looked forward to those 3-hour road trips and put a lot of thought into what we would take in the car to keep us occupied. Mom's homemade chocolate chip cookies were a required road trip snack. And sometimes, we would bring along our Connect Four and Battleship travel games. My dad had a makeshift set up in the backseat for my sister and me that we liked to call "the bed." It was a piece of plywood covered with blankets that went over the floorboard, was level with the seats, and made a large flat area where we could stretch out and sleep if needed. Because it was such a LONG trip, you know. And yes, of course, we still wore our seatbelts (*wink wink*).

I remember one year when my dad was so excited to show us a new addition to our setup. It was a small black and white TV that plugged into the cigarette lighter and only worked via antenna. We were mesmerized by this new feature. And get this. The screen that we were so excited about? The phones we carry in our pockets are bigger than that screen was. That's not really a surprise, but it's crazy to think about it now. Getting just enough reception to see the fuzzy picture appear in that tiny little square was like magic to us, and we were thrilled.

As my sister and I got older, our trips became bigger and further away. When I was 10 years old, we took the trip that every child must take at some point. Disney World! And I got to experience my first plane ride on the way there. One of my favorite things at Disney (nope, not the Princesses) was the Backstage Studio tour, where we went on a behind-the-scenes tour of some movie sets. And knowing what my interests are now, it totally makes sense that I was so fascinated by it. I was in amazement as we rode the tram through the backstage lot and saw the various movie props like the spaceship from *Flight of the Navigator* and *Herbie the Love Bug*. As our tour continued, our tram got "stuck" in the canyon just as the water began to spill down the hill toward us. That's when the director yelled, "Cut!" and we exited the live movie set. Which wasn't really live, but it's Disney, so it's the land of make-believe. The backstage tour intrigued me and created an interest in filmmaking and directing. And who knows, maybe someday I'll be a director.

The year we traveled to Colorado might be the trip that instilled adventure in me. The thrill of rafting down the rapids of the Arkansas River is something I still remember to this day. Our rafting adventure began by riding a bus up river and hearing the required safety speech before we buckled our life jackets and grabbed our oars.

The guide began the safety instructions by telling us, "We hardly ever have to use this, but we're required to tell you anyway."

We listened intently even though we didn't plan to need the information while on the river.

The instructions continued, and he told us, "In the event that you fall out, make sure to keep your feet in front of you. That way, if you were to hit a rock, your feet would hit it first instead of your head."

"Ok, got it," we thought.

"And if someone does fall out, and again this rarely happens, grab the shoulders of their life jacket and quickly push them down before yanking them back up into the raft. The momentum of pushing them down first will help," he stated.

After the briefing, we chose where each of us would sit and hopped into the raft. Our family of four was with another family of three. So, including our guide, we had eight people in the raft. Our family took their places in the front of the raft, and away we went. The splashes of the rapids were hitting our smiling faces as we laughed our way through the obstacles in the river, directed by our guide's instructions.

Midway through our adventure, our raft got stuck on a rock at a 45-degree angle. I was calm at first. Being stuck on the rock seemed like an added bonus to the adventure. Once I saw the water pooling around my feet, I quickly looked around for something to hold onto and tried using my paddle against the current to hold myself up.

"Why are we still on the rock?" I kept thinking. Looking upstream, I could see the raft behind us getting closer and hoped they were coming to help us get unstuck.

When I realized my feet were no longer touching the bottom of the raft, my heart started beating a little faster. As the water swept me away, it took me a few seconds to grasp what had just happened.

"Am I in the river? Oh my gosh, I'm in the river!"

As the river carried me further downstream, I had to remember the safety briefing we never thought we would use. In the distance, I could faintly hear someone yelling, "Keep your feet in front of you!" The roar of the rapids rang through my ears, and the cool splashes of water hit my face while I tried to catch my breath between the whitewater waves.

While floating down the river, I knew the water wasn't deep enough for my body to be completely submerged because I felt the boulders lying on the bottom of the river. My lifejacket was doing its job of keeping my head afloat; however, the rest of my body continued to drag the bottom of the shallow river. And by "rest of my body," I mean my rear end.

As the waves of rushing water continued to hit my face, I struggled to catch my breath even though I knew I was only in a few feet of water.

Why…..<*splash*>…..can't..…<*splash*>…..I…..<*splash*>..… breathe?

"What is taking so long? Why haven't they pulled me back in the raft yet?" I wondered.

I didn't know how long I had been floating downstream, but it felt like forever.

Once the raft finally caught up to me and pulled me back to safety, I noticed some of my family were in a different raft. Apparently, after I was swept out of the raft, the second raft in our group lost control and hit ours while it was still stuck on the rock. This caused my parents and my sister to all be knocked into the river as well. So, all four of us got to go swimming in the Arkansas River, and only us four. That's right, our whole family, and ONLY our family, out of 16 people, were swept down the river. You haven't experienced the Arkansas River until you've rafted it and met it face-to-face when you fell out.

Safely back in the raft, I clung to the rope handles for the remainder of the trip. As my feet hit the gravel shoreline next to the tour guide's office, and I walked with a limp after my butt had been dragged along the bottom of the river, I looked back at the water with a grin and shouted, "Let's do it again!" Unfortunately, the car ride home wasn't as fun as the river because I needed an inflatable donut to sit on after my rear end hit every boulder in the river.

Thankfully the only thing lost that day was my dad's prescription sunglasses. Not my cheap $3 neon sunglasses, nor my sister's or mom's. Just Dad's prescription ones which now lie somewhere along the bottom of the Arkansas River. But we learned a good lesson that day. Always listen to the safety briefing. Even when you think "keep your feet in front of you" sounds silly and useless!

Our whitewater experience could be why I like to do at least one adventurous thing during each trip. I believe trips are meant for experiences, whether it's rafting, hiking, ziplining, climbing bridges, or taking a polar plunge. And sometimes being adventurous means tasting local foods like crocodile or warthog. "Tastes like chicken," they say. Well, actually, the warthog tasted like ham.

Our travels continued with a road trip to New York City a few years later and a stop at Niagara Falls. That was our longest drive at that point, and I still remember being curled up in the back of the rented minivan, trying to sleep off the nauseousness.

Fun Fact. I have been known for getting car sick ever since I was a child. It happened so often that my mom carried a plastic bowl in the car just in case I decided to lose my lunch. One of those fancy plastic reusable bowls. No no, not the ones you purchase for leftovers. The kind that butter comes in. But let's be honest, those also make great bowls for leftovers. So, if you ever go on a road trip with me and I choose to drive, now you know why. And I might even have a butter bowl hidden under my seat just in case I become a passenger.

I've been known to puke in a car, on a plane, after getting off a roller coaster, on a cruise ship, at the gym when standing up too fast, and over the side of a shark diving boat. The last one left bruises on my ribs because of how many times I leaned over the rail to "feed the fish." And please don't ask me if I've tried Dramamine. Yes, of course, I take it. Every. Time. Even when flying. However, using it while flying only started after a friend's trip to Disney. As the plane prepared for landing in Florida, the turbulence started rocking us. I looked at the friend to my right and slowly reached for the barf bag in the seatback pocket. I had never (and still haven't) seen anyone use one. But at that moment, I knew it was my only choice. As the plane descended, we hit a pocket of air that jerked us down like a roller coaster topping the hill just before you lift up out of your seat. I quietly filled the bag and felt relief until we landed. As the plane came to a stop and we began making our way to the exit, I looked down and thought, "What am I supposed to do with this?" So, I casually exited the plane with my used barf bag in hand like it was a souvenir and then quickly disposed of it in the nearest trashcan.

A year after I graduated from high school, our parents took us on our first international vacation. It was our first time to see cars driving on the opposite side of the road, the first time to see traffic signs in a foreign language, and it was our first time being part of a group tour where we joined around 30 other passengers for a week-long trip together.

We were introduced to our fellow travelers when we arrived in Paris. After a welcome dinner and a good night's sleep, we boarded our charter bus, our main transportation for the next several days. Since this was our first time doing group travel, we didn't know there were tricks to finding the perfect seats. In fact, we thought we DID find the ideal seats when we stepped onto the bus that first morning.

We had just finished our European breakfast in the hotel, went upstairs to collect our carry-on luggage, said hello to our tour director holding her cartoon-like umbrella, and headed towards the bus after checking out of our room. When the bus driver opened the doors, the four of us climbed aboard, one behind the other, and found four seats together. Two seats were on one side of the aisle and two directly on the other side of the aisle so we could talk to each other. We also chose these seats because we thought if there was a point of interest on either side of the bus, we could just lean over each other to see it instead of hovering over one of our bus mates.

As we settled into our seats and tried to remember the names of the travelers we met at dinner the previous night, we eagerly turned our attention to the tour director, who stood at the front of the bus with her microphone in hand and ready to deliver instructions. After explaining the day's itinerary, she told us about the standard "seat rotation" policy.

"The what?" we thought to ourselves as we looked at each other, thinking we had succeeded in getting there early to get four seats together.

"Each day, we will rotate seats so that everyone has an opportunity to sit at the front of the bus," the tour director told us.

"No problem," we thought. "We don't mind switching seats to make it fair."

But then she explained further. We wouldn't just be switching seats, but there would be a specific order to the rotation. So, the seats you had on the first day would determine your rotation for the remainder of the trip.

"Everyone on the right side of the bus will move back two rows tomorrow. And everyone on the left side of the bus will move up two rows tomorrow," she clarified.

The four of us looked at each other and realized we would be four rows apart from each other on the second day and eight rows apart by the third day since we would rotate in a clockwise pattern.

It was comical that we thought our genius plan had worked. Fortunately, two of our fellow passengers agreed to swap sides with my parents, who would now be sitting behind my sister and me. So, each day when we boarded the bus and rotated to our new seats, they would still be sitting behind us.

We were taught a great lesson that day. And it will be the first item listed when I write my "tips and tricks" book for international travel.

While aboard the bus, our tour director also gave us a cheat sheet of frequently used words and phrases in French.

"*Bonjour*," she said with a welcoming smile.

With the list in hand, we began practicing with each other. "*Merci*," I told my sister. "It means thank you."

"*S'il vous plait* means please," my sister said in return.

My mom, who had been listening to us practice, looked at us with confusion. "CD player?" she asked.

"No, no. *See vu play* we pronounced to her right before bursting into laughter.

These are the kind of memories we made on vacations. I have no idea what the weather was like or what I was wearing. But I've never forgotten the words *s'il vous plait*.

As we explored the city of Paris, I was in awe of the landmarks we were getting to see in person. The Eiffel Tower, Notre Dame, the Arc de Triomphe, and Versailles, to name a few. It created a new fascination within me. I had never been someone who was interested in history but seeing things first-hand at the age of 19 made me want to know more about each place we went.

After France, we spent the last half of the trip in London and saw sites such as Big Ben, Tower Bridge, Windsor Castle, Westminster Abbey, and the Changing of the Guard. I still couldn't believe we were there.

Paris and London are also where I began my collection of Hard Rock Cafe pins and shot glasses. Before leaving the U.S., our travel agent requested that we pick up a souvenir for one of his clients. When he told us the client collected shot glasses from around the world, I decided it was an excellent opportunity to start my own collection.

During one of our free afternoons in London, we made our way to the Hard Rock Cafe near Hyde Park, where we learned this was the original location.

Inside the retail shop, I made my way to the shelf with the 4-inch-tall clear glasses with the red and yellow circle logo and the word "London" under them. Then I picked out a lapel pin specific to London, which went nicely with the one I purchased in Paris. And so began my collection of Hard

Rock Cafe pins and shot glasses across various states and countries.

After our trip to Europe, our family took a hiatus from traveling together because our schedules never seemed to align. But then, in 2005, we planned a trip to Washington, D.C., and we haven't missed a year since then. Yes, you understand correctly that I continued to travel with my parents and sister as an adult. It's important to us. The time spent together creates so many memories for us. Like the time we thought our luggage was lost and we would be wearing the same clothes for ten days in Italy. Or the time we were floating the canals of Venice, and our gondolier tried to convince us there were fish in the water.

"Fish, fish!" he told us as he pointed to the water. "Look!" he said with his Italian accent.

As soon as we all looked over the edge of the gondola to see the fish, he pretended we were going to tip over. We all roared with laughter.

The year following our vacation to Washington, D.C., we went outside of the USA again. The excitement leading up to it seemed different than the year we went to Paris and London, although I'm not sure why. Maybe because I realized visiting other countries could become a regular occurrence and seeing the world wouldn't just be something I heard about on TV.

Our family vacations and adventures created a desire in me to see more, so I started making my own list of places I wanted to travel. It's a list that typically grows more than it shrinks, but I hope always to be checking things off of it.

Amazing Joy

Seeing new places brings me joy because it reminds me there is so much to experience in life.

CHAPTER 3

When I look back on my younger days, I realize how grateful I am for my parents' support and their decision to let me be a kid as long as possible. I appreciate that they allowed me to set my focus on high school and not get distracted by being required to earn a paycheck. When I look back on the things my parents sacrificed for me, I realize I never thanked them enough for the way they supported me. I should probably go ahead and do that now.

Thank you, Mom and Dad, for everything you sacrificed for me when I was growing up! For example, your sacrifice of money when you went with little to make sure I had new cleats and softball pants each year. And your sacrifice of time when you made sure you were at every event to support me from the stands.

I'll never forget walking onto the field after our stretches, warmups, and team huddle and the feeling I got when I looked up to see you in the bleachers. Mom, you were always there with the VHS camera, capturing my games and memories on the field.

Melissa Kelly

Dad, you could typically be heard laughing with the other dads, and it put a warm feeling in my heart knowing you were both there.

Immediately following my high school graduation, my parents implemented the "it's time to get a job" rule. Because I was involved in so many activities up until that point, my parents and I agreed that I wouldn't have to get a part-time job as long as I was playing sports. They felt my time spent on the court and on the field was valuable and taught me lessons such as discipline and work ethic. If I had gotten a job at the same time as being on a team, my grades might have been impacted. So, they felt it was important for me to focus on grades and being a dedicated athlete.

This doesn't mean I didn't contribute to any expenses, though. For example, they agreed to help buy my car if I could pay for half of it. I'm thankful my parents didn't buy everything I asked for when I was a child because it taught me to work and save if I wanted something new. I was the kid who only spent what I had to and saved the rest. Only spending money for special occasions meant that I was accumulating a hefty savings that prepared me to split the bill with my parents when I was ready to purchase a car. The remainder of our agreement was for them to provide gas money and pay for car insurance. At 16, I didn't know just how blessed I was.

It was a rare instance for me to use birthday money or chore money on something for myself. Instead, it went into my money jar sitting next to the closet so I could watch it accumulate for just the right purchase. Perhaps a new pair of sneakers if I wanted name-brand shoes. Using my own savings made me appreciate the value of items. Therefore, when I did splurge to buy new sneakers, I kept them clean and crisp. This was the beginning of my obsession with clean sneakers. My obsession has become an inside joke with those close to me, resulting in a very popular question over the years.

"Did you get new shoes?" they would ask.

"Nope, I've had these for a year," I'd reply.

"A year? How are they still clean?" they eagerly wanted to know.

"First, you won't see me wearing them when it rains. And if unexpected sprinkles occur before I get home, then you might see me running through the parking lot in my socks," I'd explain to them with a grin.

Obsession. Addiction. Tomato. Ta-mah-toe.

It probably sounds like I was spoiled. And I was. But not to the extent that I didn't appreciate what I had. Did I have new clothes every year for school? I sure did. But they were never name-brand, and those kinds of life lessons have stuck with me through my adult years. I don't feel like I have to have the best of something or the latest and greatest. And if I buy something new, I keep it until it's on its last legs. Just ask my friends who made fun of me for having a 4-year-old iPhone. That's ancient in iPhone years!

When I began looking for summer jobs after high school, I avoided the fast-food locations and chose not to fill out an application at any of them. There was something about going home and smelling like food I didn't want. It's one thing to like the taste of French fries, but bathing in the fragrance all day is another thing.

"You should apply at the Supercenter," a close friend told me.

"That's a good idea. It checks my requirement box of not being a fast-food restaurant. And being a cashier sounds fun." I replied.

I would have even been okay with stocking shelves, so I went for it.

I was excited when I received a call about scheduling an interview at Walmart. But my excitement quickly faded when I was told what department I would be interviewing for. I found out it would be in the deli...frying chicken. Let me repeat that. In the deli...frying chicken. That sounds a lot like fast food to me! Which was my number one requirement of where I DIDN'T want to work. But it was the only place I had heard back from, so I accepted the job.

I remember my first day very well. Actually, I don't remember the day at work as much as I do the drive home and the moment I walked into the house. When I got home each night, my parents would get a whiff of the grease smell as I walked in the door. It's funny how the smell of fried chicken is so different when you're about to eat it than it is when you're wearing it. In addition to wearing the smell, my shoes were covered in grease because as we took the chicken out of the fryer; the basket would drip and create a slip-n-slide between the fryer and the counter. Those became my work shoes for two reasons. 1) I wouldn't be able to wear them anywhere else because people would smell me coming from a mile away, and 2) I CAN'T STAND wearing dirty shoes.

The next few days of my first job were the same. Fry chicken. Smell like grease. Repeat. Standing in front of the nauseating hot fryers all day gave me a headache, so I quickly discovered the walk-in cooler was a great place to cool off. Sometimes we would take an extra-long time finding the potato salad in the cooler just so we could let the sweat dry a little before returning to the sauna.

It wasn't very long after I started my first job when I began begging my parents to let me quit. But I should have known their response because they never let me quit anything I started. Whether it was a new sport, band, Girl Scouts, etc. It wasn't that I had to do these things forever. But if I started something, I had to stick it out until the season ended or the year was over. So, I agreed to stick it out for the summer (since that's when I thought my "season" with Walmart would end.)

As fall rolled around and I was about to begin my first year of college, I was hoping I wouldn't have to continue working in the deli. I was attempting to be a walk-on for the softball team in college, and I knew if I made the team, we would be back to my parent's rule of sports coming before a job. Unfortunately, my days as a softball catcher didn't continue past high school. And the unfortunate part of that meant I had to keep smelling like chicken. And if you think this made the men flock towards me and drool, you would be wrong. Maybe I should have cooked bacon all day. I bet that would have drawn their attention.

As I continued my part-time job, I began learning a key element that still sticks with me today. Customer service. As a shy teenager, I was not in the habit of talking to strangers. But being in the service industry changed that very quickly. I was forced to make eye contact, ew. And I had to learn to speak to people as soon as eye contact was made. It taught my 18-year-old introverted self a lot. In the first days of my job, I would just stare at customers as they approached the counter, hoping they would say something first. I quickly learned it was part of my job to speak to them first.

"Hi, what can I get for you today?" I would ask.

"I'll take a pound of sliced turkey," the customer would reply.

And just like there is with almost anything you order, I asked the follow-up question, "How would you like that sliced?"

"Thin sliced," they would tell me.

Yes, even though the chicken is what I can still smell to this day and what I couldn't eat for years, I also learned how to use a meat/cheese slicer without losing any fingers. I became skilled at knowing the precise position to place the dial on the slicer to get the perfect thickness for their desired deli slices. Well, maybe not perfect because adjustments were often needed after a quick customer preview. We got good at knowing how much "a tiny bit more" is and the correct number for "shredded" turkey. Knowing when to stop slicing to make exactly one pound became another skill. Yes, of course, I put these amazing skills on my resume.

Every brand of turkey, ham, and cheese, along with salads and items at the chicken counter, had a 4-digit number we had to key in, which would then spit out a small white label with the price. We had a cheat sheet printed out and hanging next to the registers, but after working there all summer, I memorized many of the numbers. We would rattle off the numbers to each other as a quiz to see who could get the most right. So, it's a good thing I didn't have a lot of PINs back then because I would have been typing in pepper jack cheese when trying to access the ATM.

Due to my college schedule, I typically worked evenings and weekends. Evenings were my jam because that's when the fun happened. Although I think my co-workers might say it's because I brought the fun, but we'll let them admit that themselves. Since there weren't as many customers in the late evening, we usually listened to music and just laughed and had an all-around good time. It's probably a good thing I can't remember everything we did. What happens in the deli, stays in the deli.

As the holidays arrived each year, we would get order after order for boxes of chicken and deli trays. For Christmas, we would get so many orders for meat and cheese trays that we had to set up tables and bring in extra people to help. It was a multi-day event and is probably to blame for my ability to fold deli meat in my sleep.

I continued to work in the deli while I attended college, where I was working on a degree in Computer Information

Systems. During my junior year, I had to begin deciding where I would complete my summer internship. I applied to three companies in our area with IT departments because staying close to home was important to me. My college professor, who led the internship program, suggested I apply at the Walmart Home Office. I think I had only been to Arkansas once in my life, so applying to be an intern in Arkansas wasn't even on my radar. My professor thought I had a good chance of getting accepted since I already worked for the company at the local Supercenter.

I took a chance and applied for Walmart's IT department. I was surprised when they wanted to do an interview. While considering the offer, I had to decide if I wanted to move away from home for the summer. This was not in my plans because I enjoyed being around family, and since I was still living in my hometown, I could stay in contact with most of my friends from high school. But I knew this would be a good opportunity that would look good on my resume and allow me to continue working at the Supercenter once my internship was over. So, I accepted the offer to intern at the Walmart Home Office.

I don't do well with change, so saying goodbye to my co-workers for the summer was difficult. Saying goodbye to family and friends was also hard, but knowing I wasn't going very far helped eliminate the sadness and turn it into excitement.

I moved in with two other girls for the summer; it was my first time having roommates. The 2-bedroom house we were given to rent consisted of '60s & '70s décor and was in the middle of a retirement community. We were 20 minutes outside of downtown, where we worked, and 40 minutes away from weekend activities. But it was still better than being crammed into an apartment for the summer.

The drive from my hometown to my rental took about an hour. This is partly what sold me on the internship because I realized I could drive to Arkansas on Sunday evening, work Monday through Friday, and then drive back home to Missouri on Friday evening and still enjoy my weekends with my family and friends over the summer. This allowed me to attend birthday parties, baseball games, pool parties, and 4th of July events with family. I only slightly regret not staying in Arkansas over the weekends to build more friendships among the interns. I never felt like I was missing out on things in Arkansas. However, the thought of missing out on family events saddened me. During that era, I found maintaining old friendships easier than building new ones because my social anxiety was calling the shots. I wanted to be in comfortable and familiar situations and feared anything new.

Traveling home each weekend to stay with my parents is something I look back on now, and I thank God for the opportunity. I realize now He had a plan for me not spending weekends in Arkansas because time spent with family is valuable and much shorter than we might realize. And God is the only one who knew just how short that time would be.

Being an intern for the world's largest retailer was incredible to me. I was a little star-struck at first, knowing I was walking through the halls of a successful corporation. And I think I was a little giddy when I got my new badge. My name and picture under the word "Wal-Mart."

The IT department was growing, and within a year of working there, it was larger than the population of my hometown. And that was just one department. It was so crazy to me. For a small-town girl still in college, it was mind-blowing to be there.

During my first project assignment, I struggled to get a specific piece of code working.

"Try reaching out to the Microsoft representative," my mentor suggested.

"You mean I can just call Microsoft and ask them?" I asked with a stunned reaction.

Not only could I call and ask them, but they were in the building, and someone came to my desk to discuss the issue. Mind-blown again. These things seem like no big deal now, but at the time, I couldn't stop grinning about everything I was part of.

My time as an intern allowed me to develop friendships that would follow me throughout my career. And some of those friendships were developed through our office antics. One particular event still gets talked about over 20 years later.

It started innocent and small. With the help of a few co-workers, we removed everything from Judy's desk, placed it on her chair, and enclosed it with plastic wrap. Once the contents of her desk, including her scissors, were wrapped like a present on top of her chair, we then used plastic wrap around her entire cubicle entrance and the roof of it so she couldn't reach her desk. Keep in mind her scissors were deep inside all of this. Oh, and did I mention we put confetti on top of the plastic wrap so it would create a huge mess when it was cut down?

After finally gaining access to her cubicle and desk, she began plotting her revenge against me. But I already had my next step in mind. When it was my turn to prank Judy again, I waited until she went to lunch, removed a few keys on her keyboard, and rearranged the letters. I honestly wasn't sure if this would work because she could be someone who doesn't need to look at her keyboard to type. As she returned from lunch, I patiently waited at my desk in front of hers and listened for any sign of a reaction. I thought it was a bust at first.

And then I heard faint sounds of defeat and mummers of "what is going on?"

I waited a few minutes and walked around the corner. "What happened?" I asked her.

Judy replied, "Either my keyboard isn't working, or I took too much Tylenol at lunch."

I couldn't keep a straight face when she said she thought she had taken too much medicine for a headache. So, I confessed.

But the prank war didn't end there. It was now Friday afternoon, and Judy waited until I went to a meeting before executing her next move. She took one of the wheels off the bottom of my chair to make it lean and wobble. After my meeting, I returned to my desk, and as I pulled out my chair to sit down, I immediately noticed it leaning. I chuckled. Since everyone else had left for the day, I realized I had the upper hand in being able to tell my side of the story on Monday morning. And I had ALL WEEKEND to come up with my side of the story.

Monday morning rolled around, and it was the start of the week when I was supposed to play in a big corporate softball game. And guess who arrived to work with her arm in a sling? That's right. Me.

When I turned to walk down our aisle, Judy immediately noticed the sling. "What happened?" she asked.

"I fell out of my chair because of the missing wheel, which caused me to dislocate my shoulder," I told her.

Her jaw dropped. "You're just messing with me," she claimed.

I was absolutely messing with her and had already told all of our co-workers to go along with it. We had her convinced that I had indeed dislocated my shoulder and wouldn't be able to play in the softball game, which I had been looking forward to all summer. And just like that, the prank war was over, and I was declared the winner.

The corporate softball game I had been looking forward to was initiated by the interns when we stood up in a company-wide meeting and challenged the executive team to a game of softball. And by the executive team, I mean the CEO, COO, CIO, etc. All the Chiefs and their teams! It was unlikely that the executives would turn us down because we issued the challenge in front of a packed auditorium. They accepted the challenge.

Before the interns left for the summer and went back to school, we were given a lasting memory of being the first class of interns to play a softball game against the Executive team of the world's largest retailer. It was a game for the history books because it became a tradition for at least the next 15 years.

With my parents in the stands, as I said before, they never missed a game, they watched me and the other interns take the field. The interns were ahead in the fourth inning, and that's when the game got interesting. The executives sent in their backup team, none of which were executives but instead a team of athletes who played in a league together. The new players kept scoring run after run because the interns were unable to stop them. And one by one, the interns began sneaking into the outfield to help out their teammates. I can neither confirm nor deny that the interns had 20 players on the field by the time the inning was over. The executives, or should I say the ringers, eventually pulled ahead to win the game. But who really won? It depends on who you ask. The interns beat the executives, but the ringers beat the interns. That's my story, and I'm sticking to it.

After the game, the executives were kind enough to meet the interns and take pictures. I thought taking a picture with the company's top executives would be fun, so I waited for each of them to be available. And then, on the last day of my internship, I walked onto Executive Row and had each of them sign the print of the photo we had taken after the game. I still can't believe I was able to walk in and ask them to sign it. Mind blown yet again.

Before my last day as an intern ended, I received an offer to return full-time once I completed my degree. As a college student on the verge of graduating, I was thrilled to know already what my next move was. Accepting the job offer took away a lot of stress, and now all I had to worry about was finding a place to live.

Apartment hunting and buying furniture for the first time was exciting. My mom accompanied me throughout the looking and purchasing process. I wondered if she was sad that I was moving or if she was jumping for joy that I was finally leaving the house. Since I had lived at home during college, this would be my first time to actually move out. Although I don't know if I ever really left because I visited home A LOT. However, I found a card she sent me about a year after I moved to Arkansas, and I can now confirm she missed me. I've since had it engraved onto glass, and her sweet reminder sits on my nightstand.

My career in Information Systems began the same way my internship did. On a team. And this team became like family. It's the way we operated at that time in the company. We worked together, we ate lunch together, we spent weekends together, we celebrated birthdays and holidays together, and we had fun together. Stressful times call for fun, and I can assure you we had a lot of fun.

I recall one night when we were working late on a project. It was probably after 10 PM, and we were getting loopy from exhaustion. A teammate of mine had a stuffed gopher on his desk. Yes, a toy gopher that stood around a foot tall. We decided the gopher needed to make an appearance to our manager, who was down the hall working away. So, the gopher became a puppet and began dancing across the top of her office and peeking around the corner to scare her. It worked.

Before we left for the night, we hid the gopher in her office. Hiding the gopher became a regular thing, and we would put it in a different location each time. I even made the gopher a name badge so he felt like part of the team. His name was so fitting too. Gopher. The gopher stuck around as the years went by, even as we changed teams. And sometimes, when least expected, he would show up in that same manager's office to let her know we hadn't forgotten her.

It's things like this that made me love my job.

But then there are the parts of the job that drained us.

Having long days and short weekends was a frequent occurrence for us. It was wearing on our health and our relationships. But we powered through it because we felt invested in the company. We felt like the company cared about us, so we wanted to do our part to make the company succeed. Whether it was soon-to-be-outdated software that needed to be updated to keep working or a government compliance project that came with a quick deadline. Project after project, we were there doing our part.

It wasn't just the projects with potential fines we had to worry about, though. We also had to work on customer requests for new features and fix anything that broke throughout the week; sometimes, this meant even LONGER hours. Because occasionally, servers would go down. And sometimes, okay, just one instance, the server would go down at the same time every night. We couldn't figure out what was causing it. Since the server was in another country, we couldn't be there to see what was happening, so a security camera was installed. When we found the culprit, we were stunned. The cleaning crew unplugged the server every night to PLUG IN THEIR VACUUM. This definitely provided a good laugh… and a good story.

Another story of a server going down is one I recall very vividly because I was the person who took the report from the customer about their application not working.

"We're getting an error," they told me

After looking at the error they described, I responded, "It looks like it can't reach the server. Let me try to ping it." I paused as I tried to log into the server. "I think the server is down. Let me call operations," I told them as I began contacting our server operations team.

Once I got the server support team on the phone, they informed me there had been a request to update the server, and it appeared someone had copied over all of our data. "We'll have to restore it from backup," they told me.

My jaw dropped. "What did you just say?" I asked. The person on the other end of the phone had no idea that the server they were referring to WAS THE BACKUP, and they just wiped out all of our data which took months to build.

This server was not a normal scenario. Usually, two servers looked exactly the same, so if one went down, the applications would default to the second server. Each "box" was a mirror image of the other one. However, in this instance, our data was so big that we needed very large and expensive servers to hold it. When the project was started, the decision was made to begin with one server and store the backup within the same place.

The "update" that was being done on the server at the time of the error was creating our mirrored copy of the server so that we would now have our A and B copies of the server.

Instead of copying data from the A server to the B server, they mistakenly copied the EMPTY B server to the A and, in turn, wiped out all of our data.

At that moment, I knew we were in for a long weekend. But how were we going to rebuild months' worth of work in a matter of hours or days? It took about a week, but we miraculously pulled it off. Amazing things can happen when it's a multiple-team effort.

Even though the server being erased was an issue we would have preferred to avoid, it was a perfect example of teamwork and hard work. It was a time when we came together to make sure the job got done and then celebrated afterward. It's one of the times when our customers dropped off a basket of goodies because they knew we would put in a lot of hours during the rebuild. My favorite thing in the basket was a barrel of monkeys. Yes, a green barrel of red plastic monkeys that one could find in the toy section of the store. Anytime someone walked by my desk, they would re-arrange the red monkeys hanging together by their arms and then place them in a new location in my cubicle. The thing that wasn't in the basket, though, was the caramel brownies I requested. I'm still waiting for those!

There were many times when working on a support issue or a project that we went home just in time to change clothes and be back at our desks for the start of the next day. I remember one night while working late, our customers were leaving around 7:00 PM and joked that they better not see us in the same clothes the following day. When the customers arrived the next morning, there we were, in the same spot and in the same clothes as when they saw us the night before. We had never left.

Those were stressful times, and like a lot of other corporate jobs, we saw our co-workers more than we did our families. Was it tough to adhere to the deadlines? Absolutely! Was it worth it? I can say it defined my character and work ethic, and those are things I'm thankful for.

CHAPTER 4

One area of my life where it's sometimes harder to choose joy is being single. As a high school teenager, I began dreaming of the day I would walk down the aisle. I imagined the guests who would be there, the songs that would play, the pictures from my childhood that would rotate in the slideshow loop at the reception, and the friends I would have standing beside me in my bridal party. I didn't know who would place the ring on my finger and say, "I Do," but I knew the qualities I was looking for. Maybe that's where I went wrong. I had high expectations that would have been hard for any man to meet.

Following the dream wedding was a list of names I began creating for our children. After all, it would take a lot of planning to find a name that wasn't already taken, considering the number of relatives I have. And one day, after our children were grown, the dreams of traveling the world together would come to pass.

The unfilled dreams of a wedding day turned into loneliness over the years. It's no fun to sit at home alone on a Saturday night and stare at your reflection beaming back at you on the TV screen. And before you say that you'd love to have a night alone in the house without any kids around, let me remind you there is a difference between being alone and loneliness. Being alone is the physical state of being by yourself. Loneliness reaches the emotional side and is the feeling of sadness caused by not having someone around.

The loneliness turned into feeling left out, a feeling which began in high school when I saw my friends walking around in their boyfriends' letter jackets, and I felt hopeless because I was wearing my own. But in high school, at least I had other people around me who also weren't dating. The older I got, the more I became the minority in the dating world, which led to me being the 3rd wheel.

It's something I've become used to, and maybe I'm not normal, but I actually like it. Well, let me be specific. I don't LIKE being the 3rd wheel, but I will take that over arguing with myself about what to watch on tv. If you are someone who is married and/or has children, don't be afraid to include your single friends. They may tell you no, but give them a chance to say no rather than assume they don't want to be the odd man out.

My feelings of being left out turned into embarrassment. Being past the age when it's *normal* to get married often makes me feel embarrassed because it feels like "everyone" is married but me. Even though that isn't true, it's still the feeling I get when sitting by myself at a baseball game or concert.

The embarrassment turned into hurt. Being hurt by someone who isn't meant for you is one thing. But being hurt by people who don't even intend to hurt you is another thing. I'm referring to the people who don't ask me if I'm dating anyone. Why don't they ask me? Do they think I'm not worthy of a relationship? Why don't they try to set me up with anyone? Do they think I'm not good enough? I have been in many group settings where it's another single person and me, and the conversation tends to be about setting up the other person and telling them they are too pretty to be single.

"Hello, I'm sitting right here," I want to yell at them.

Are they saying only pretty people deserve to be in relationships? I've been described as "pretty fun," "pretty athletic," "pretty dependable," "pretty funny," and "pretty kind," but never just "pretty." So, if only pretty people deserve to be in relationships, then I guess I know why I'm still single.

The hurt turned into being scared. Since I fear I will never know what it's like to be loved, the thought of dying alone scares me also. With no spouse or children of my own, I often worry there will be no one to take care of me when I'm old or if I get sick. I imagine myself being in a nursing home with no one around me when I take my last breath. Death doesn't scare me. But dying alone does. Who will be there to create my funeral arrangements? Who will visit my grave and leave flowers? Since I won't be leaving behind children or grandchildren, who will wonder what I was like at their age?

Serious relationships have never been in my cards. It's something I question on a frequent basis when I'm having prayer time with God. And because the relationships never turn into anything serious, I'm scared that I will never know what it feels like to be loved romantically.

Looking back on my life, there are ones I dated, ones I wanted to date, and ones I shouldn't have dated. It's the ones I shouldn't have dated that I have to remember when drowning in my tears of singleness. I have to remind myself that I could be married to someone who is abusive, someone who is a cheater, someone who was not in it for the right reasons, or someone who is a narcissist and always making me wonder about our relationship because things would always be on his terms. I would have wondered when he'd be home because his timeline was the only one that mattered. And the narcissist would have made me feel like a crazy person because every time I caught him in a lie, he would try to turn the blame on me. I have to remind myself that being single is better than settling for a marriage I hate coming home to. If I'm going to take the long way home from work, it's going to be to avoid an empty house, not to avoid my spouse.

Being single has brought on new feelings throughout each stage of life.

Singleness in your teens is hanging out with your girls and having slumber parties. It's going to the movies with your friends because half of them are single too. It's finding a prom date at the last minute because he didn't have one either. And for me, it was sitting in my room with the green shag carpet on Saturday nights, listening to the countdown on the radio because what else was I supposed to do during high school when my friends were on dates and I didn't have one? I sat patiently, waiting for just the right moment to hear that very first note of the top slow songs, and with a racing heart, I quickly pressed the record button on the cassette player. Once the song ended, I dashed to the player to rewind the tape, only to discover that I missed the first few notes of the song's introduction. Creating my own mixtape was my journey through teenage love. Song introductions weren't the only thing I missed out on during those years.

I wanted to be on a date with my current crush and dreamed that our song would be "Keeper of the Stars" because it described a love that was meant to be. Not to be confused with the song "Someone Else's Star"…which is apparently where I was wishing.

Singleness in college is watching your friends start their families. It's attending every activity on campus to find "the one." It's listening to the queen of sappy love songs on the radio while driving home from night classes. She played just the right songs to make me dream of falling in love. I would listen to each caller and couldn't wait to call the request line once I found the love of my life. That was over 20 years ago. I still have never called the request line.

Singleness as an adult is grilling steaks for two and having leftovers. It's paying more to travel because you get charged a single supplement. It's coming home after a long day with good news to share but nobody to share it with. It's crying over a sad movie and not having anyone to wipe away your tears. It's not having a plus-one to attend events with. It's not having anyone to wear matching pj's with on the annual Christmas card. It's a status that's being placed on you because there must be something "wrong" with you since you have never been married. It's watching your friends' families grow, and now their children are having kids. It's knowing you'll never have grandchildren to spoil. It's wanting to run away and move somewhere where no one knows you. Because then at least you could tell yourself the reason you're not married is that nobody's around except the owners of the Airbnb you're staying in.

Singleness when choosing joy is continuing to live life while still desiring more. It's not being afraid to do things alone because you'd rather buy a single concert ticket than no ticket at all. It's going for a walk to admire the cotton candy sunset. It's finding the perfect destination to travel to and BOOKING THE TRIP. It's not letting your marital status halt your life. And it's not settling for someone who isn't meant for you.

I know that every relationship isn't perfect, and relationships don't "fix" what is missing. I will also say that I have managed to create a very good life for myself and that I choose to live a life full of joy even though it hurts not to have something I've always wanted. But living a life full of joy doesn't mean the desire for a family goes away. It just means I've learned to find things in my life to be happy about and not focus on the negative stuff.

Having unmet desires for a family and having joy CAN co-exist. I would hate to sit at home and be miserable when there are so many options for enjoying life. I want to see the world and create new memories. And spend time with friends and family because I crave relationships. Quality time is one of my love languages. And quality time for me sometimes just means being in the same room with people. There doesn't even have to be any talking, although that drives some people crazy. If I'm in the same room or same car with you and I don't say a word for an extended period of time, it doesn't mean something is wrong. It's just me enjoying the presence of another human being.

Regardless of who we are and what our situation is, we can find pros and cons in everything we do. The things I see as pros are the things you see as cons. And sometimes, the things you see as pros are the things I see as cons.

Con: The house is quiet.
Pro: The house is quiet.

Con: I don't have anyone to cook for me.
Pro: I don't have to cook for anyone.

Con: I don't have anyone to check on me if I'm not home at a certain time.
Pro: I don't have anyone to answer to if I want to stay out later.

Con: I don't have another person's income as a backup if my business is slow.

Pro: I can spend money where I choose to spend it.

Con: I don't have anyone to spoil me on my birthday.

Pro: I don't have to spoil anyone on their birthday. Actually, I like spoiling people on their birthdays, so I guess that's not a pro after all.

Recognizing the pros has allowed me to choose joy throughout my journey. We have to live our own journey and find ways to appreciate the path we've been placed on. I could complain about being single, and I have definitely done that a time or two. And when I did, I was miserable because all I could see was the negative side of it. I've learned to find the good in it and have found joy through it, even though it's not what I intended or wanted.

For whatever reason, God has put me on a path of singleness. Maybe one day I'll understand why, but right now, I still haven't figured it out. And when it comes to marriage, I'm still hoping that His answer is "not yet" versus "no," but only time will tell. In the meantime, I'm learning to live life to the fullest rather than sitting around waiting and wishing my life was different. Although I will admit, it has taken A LOT of work to get to this point of trusting and believing in His plan. Just because it's not my plan doesn't mean it can't be a good one.

Sometimes our life doesn't turn out the way we had it planned in our minds. Those plans we made as a child or teenager when we thought we had it all figured out. I knew exactly what I wanted my life to look like, and I knew the steps I had to take to get there. Some of those steps were within my control. Like working hard to get into college. But some of those steps I couldn't control even if I wanted to. Like, make someone fall in love with me.

But just because our life doesn't turn out like we think we wanted it to doesn't mean we can't have a great life anyway. It took me a long time to realize this, and I knew I would never be happy until I said, "Ok, God, I'll do it your way." His plans look so much different than mine did. I never expected to still be single at this age. And I always thought I would have a family and kids of my own. But instead, He gave me new dreams and plans I never imagined. Despite the disappointments, I still recognize that it's a life worth living for. A life that I can hopefully use to inspire others.

CHAPTER 5

When I was fresh out of college and moving out of my childhood home, I was excited to see what the world had waiting for me. I was moving to a new state, living on my own for the first time, and starting a corporate job. All of these things were exciting to me as a young 22-year-old because I saw these things as a potential for meeting my future husband. After all, starting a family was high on my list of things to do next, and since I hadn't met him in my hometown or while going to college, I thought the reason God provided a job for me in another state was for me to meet my soulmate.

While continuing to focus on my career, I still couldn't help but wonder, "when?" When am I going to meet my future husband?

My friends were settling down and having kids, but I was still living the single life. I began asking the dreaded questions like "what's wrong with me?" and "why not me,

God?" These questions stuck with me for many years…and continue to stick with me.

As someone who has never been married, I often hear the same clichés over and over again.

"Maybe you're too picky." You're right. What's the point of integrity anyway?

"There's plenty of fish in the sea." There are also plenty of mosquitos in the air, but that doesn't mean I want them living in my house.

"Maybe you're called to be single." Girl, I've met your husband. Maybe you were called to be single, too, but you didn't answer that day.

"Just be patient. It's worth the wait when you find him." Yeah, thanks for the advice. You got married at 19 and only dated ONE person in your lifetime. Please tell me again about patience.

"Jesus was single too." So, I guess that means YOU don't want to be like Jesus since YOU are married!

"It doesn't matter what he looks like as long as he treats you right." Thanks, and say hello to your GQ husband for me.

"Love will find you when you stop looking." But wait, don't we always find things in the last place we looked?

"Have you tried online dating?" Have you tried walking on a bed of nails while blindfolded and holding a scalding cup of coffee? Because it's as painful as that. Please get back to me once you have.

And my favorite, *"You have to put yourself out there."* Put myself where? On a billboard?!

Outside of the clichés, I have been repeatedly reminded that God's timing is perfect. Which is usually followed by "You don't need a man because God loves you." While I know and believe God truly does love me, it is far from the same thing. Yes, His love is greater than earthly love, but it's still not the same thing as having someone embrace you when your life just got turned upside down, or you had a bad day at work.

I've also heard on many occasions the words "I wonder what is wrong with them?" when someone around me sees a person over 40 who has never been married. "They must play a lot of video games" seems to be their reasoning for that person never being married, which is their subtle way of saying "they are a loser." I don't sit around playing video games, but does never being married make me a loser? On second thought, I do love a good game of Super Mario Bros., so I guess I'm a loser, also.

I remember being in England the first time I ever saw a roundabout. It was intriguing and entertaining to watch the cars travel around it. I thought it was the most fascinating traffic circle and wondered why we didn't have them in the U.S. And then years later, my sister and I were elated when we saw one in the U.S. for the first time. Yes, we get excited about the silliest things. The joy of seeing a roundabout in the U.S. quickly faded when we realized our residents don't know how to drive on one, unlike the British, who are pros at it.

As you enter the circle, if you end up on the inside lane, you might be unsure how to get out of the circle, therefore, you just keep going around and around. Sometimes I feel like that's how the single life is for me. I feel like I'm stuck in a roundabout that I don't know how to get out of, and therefore I just keep circling with no end in sight.

Being stuck in the circle of singleness means I don't have anyone to check on the loud noise I just heard outside or to check on me when I'm sick. It means I don't have anyone to take the trash out when it's raining, cold, or snowing. And it means I don't have anyone to comfort me when I'm sad or welcome me with a warm embrace after a long week.

But on the other hand, being stuck in the circle of singleness has its advantages and has allowed me to be spontaneous. I can take off on weekend trips whenever I want to, and I don't have to worry about what someone else wants for dinner. I get to choose what to watch on TV from any room in the house, or all rooms in the house at the same time if I want. I've never actually done that. Okay, maybe once.

If I want to leave the windows open all night and let the cool air of spring fill the bedroom until it's 67 degrees in the house WHILE the ceiling fan is on, then I'm able to do that without asking permission from anyone.

I've had some great friends over the years who have included me in their families and treated me like part of theirs. I've watched their kids grow up, and I became an honorary aunt to them.

Being invited and included in other people's families and being able to spend time in the home of others rather than be alone in my quiet house brings me joy.

My ongoing single life created an independence within me because I don't like to be a burden on others, and asking for help is one of the hardest things for me to do. Therefore, I have learned to become very self-sufficient. But not because I want to be. It's because I have to be.

Living alone and being single forces independence because sometimes I find it easier to tackle a problem or project by myself instead of bothering a friend. I would rather hold up a curtain rod with my head as I measure with one hand and hold the hammer in the other than call someone to help me with a small and easy task. Although it's only small and easy if more than one person is assigned to the task. But try to do it by yourself, and it's now taken an hour, two lost nails because you dropped them while holding the nails and the hammer in the same hand, and multiple holes in the wall because you can't reach far enough to measure correctly. And if you think that's amusing, you should watch me put together an office desk. Did you know it takes arms AND legs to accomplish that task?

My independence took the forefront when I became a homeowner at the age of 23. I had been renting a 2-bedroom apartment the first summer I lived away from home and had the company of a summer roommate until she went back to school.

Living on the first floor of an apartment complex had the advantage of making it easier to carry furniture when moving in. But it had the disadvantage of living under tenants who sounded like they wore bricks on their shoes.

After a year of apartment life, I had had enough of it. I was ready to find something else to rent and wanted to look at duplexes so I could have a garage. I didn't know anything about real estate, so when a friend told me it was a seller's market and a good time to buy a house, I didn't know what that meant. Nor did I want to buy a house. I was only 23 years old, so why would I buy a house? I thought people only took that step when they were starting a family. And since it was just me, it didn't make sense.

I began looking for duplexes, and on a whim, decided to see what kind of houses were available. I quickly noticed my friend was right and that it was a good time to buy because prices were so low. So, I changed courses. And now I was on a house hunt.

I think I was a realtor's dream because I had no must-haves and no deal breakers. I'm not saying I loved every house, but it was such a new and exciting experience that I was happy with generally all of them.

The first one I made an offer on was just down the road from my friend. I didn't care for the small living room, but there were no houses behind it, so I liked the idea of having no neighbors behind me. Other than the cows, who would have been my backyard neighbors. But I got beat out by a different offer.

The next house I liked was in the same vicinity, and I was focusing on this city because it was between my work to the north and entertainment to the south. There was nothing special I liked or disliked about this house. So, I chose to make an offer on it based on location. And again, they accepted a higher offer.

The final house was one I had already looked at and passed on. They had dropped the price, so I gave it another look. And that's when I remembered the back porch. It was huge, and it was covered. Take my money because I want the porch! It was also facing an open field, and I loved that I would have room for patio furniture and a grill. To my delight, they accepted the offer.

At 23 years old, I was now a homeowner. Twenty-three! That was completely unexpected and unplanned. Some of my friends were having babies at 23. But I bought a house. It's funny how God can put things in your path that you never intended to happen. We usually see Him do that with bad things, like an illness, but have you ever stopped to think about the good things He has done for you that you never predicted?

As a new homeowner, I often asked myself why I took such a big step. What if I met my future husband, and we wanted to buy a different house together? But the even bigger question I asked myself was, why did I buy a house if I'm only going to stay in Arkansas for 5 years? I didn't plan on staying any longer than that because I still wanted to live near my hometown. Spoiler alert, I've now lived in Arkansas for 22 years. I have a feeling God is laughing at my 5-year prediction.

Being independent also means that I began enjoying outings by myself. I have been known to go to movies alone, baseball games, nature walks, concerts, and on rare occasions, maybe even to a restaurant.

Dining alone or going on other outings alone is not something I prefer, but I also don't want to miss out on life. It takes a lot of courage to do those things alone, and it's not something that came easy for me. Did I feel stupid the first few times when walking in alone? Absolutely. I felt like everyone was staring at me, and it made me self-conscious. It took me a while to realize that nobody cares, and they aren't staring at you as much as you think they are. And if they are staring at you, just turn around, wave to them, and own it. Be proud of your independence!

The more years that went by while being single, the more frustrated I got. I wanted more out of life and thought I needed my own family to have that. If I wanted to buy a bigger house surrounded by a few acres, I thought I needed a family for that. Or if I wanted to travel to far-off destinations, I thought I needed others with me. Or, if I wanted to start a new career and possibly go back to school, I thought I needed someone else to help support me during the process of starting something new. There were also times when I just wanted someone to comfort me during the depressing times or walk beside me during the heartbreaking times. Ok, I still want those last two things, but I have found workarounds that fill the gap in the meantime. Like great friends by my side and a fantastic counselor who talks me through things.

Something else I have had to learn to do alone is holidays, which can be really tough to attend by myself. I have an amazing family, and we generally spend every holiday together, so I'm grateful not to be alone on holidays. But when I say I don't want to attend events by myself, it's because I still wish I had my own family, a spouse, and children. I've longed for the day when I would get to wake up on Christmas morning and watch my own kids open their presents with the same excitement my parents had when they watched us open our Nintendo Entertainment System or when I was instructed to walk to the front porch to see my new red 10-speed bike waiting for me. And I hoped that someday, I would get to spoil my grandchildren on Christmas. But it doesn't appear this is something that will happen in my future, and I'm still learning to process that unfulfilled desire.

Not all holidays give me the same feeling, but almost all of them are a trigger of some kind for me. Meaning if I don't prepare myself ahead of time and recognize the things that could affect me emotionally, then when they happen, I go down a hole of depression and possibly anxiety. And how do I prepare myself? Let's take one of the most dreaded holidays for singles as an example. Good ole Valentine's Day. For many people, February 14th is a day of celebration and a day of love. But for myself, it's typically not a day I look forward to. When you are single, it's not just one day but more like a whole week leading up to it that you have to avoid. If you walk into any store at all, it's usually an entire month of avoidance because of all the holiday items on the shelves. And you will quickly notice the color red has vomited all over every aisle. I like red, but I cringe when I see it in February.

Seeing the candy, cards, balloons, and stuffed animals at the store gives me the feeling of being punched in the stomach. It's that in-your-face moment that says, "hey, don't forget about this day that makes you feel like you don't mean anything." Being single is one thing. But being reminded I'm single is another category, and that's exactly what Valentine's Day does to me. It's a reminder that I haven't gotten that long-awaited dream of having a family. It's a reminder that loneliness stinks. It's a reminder that I have to do life alone.

So rather than dread Valentine's Day or any other holiday that gets me down, I like to figure out ways to not think about it and maybe even some ways to enjoy it. Sometimes I plan a girls' night and have fun with friends instead of sitting at home alone. And on occasion, I have even bought myself a present on Valentine's Day, because who doesn't need an excuse to buy a new CD (yes, that's old school, but I did it once).

I will tell you something NOT to do on Valentine's Day, though. And while I don't know this from experience, I know someone who does. DO NOT, I repeat, DO NOT, under any circumstances, think that you are going to treat yourself to a spa day to avoid the reminders of what day it is. Because if you do, you will be greeted by all the couples at the spa who thought it would be fun to get a massage together.

Would you believe even Halloween can trigger feelings of loneliness? Over the years, I've missed out on dressing up in cute couple's costumes and taking my own kids trick-or-treating. But I've also been blessed to tag along with friends when they take their kids around the neighborhood. Being with my friends and their children on Halloween is on the list of things that bring me joy!

So, you've heard how I handle outings and holidays while living the single life. But what about the desire to have my own children? Knowing that I'll never have a biological child is an ache in my heart that won't go away. Knowing I will never give my parents the gift of grandchildren. Realizing I'll never know what my mini-me will look like and whether or not they will carry the red-headed gene. Never finding out if I do indeed carry the trait for twins that runs on both sides of my family. Knowing I won't have daughters who share the same middle name as so many others in the family. Realizing I don't have anyone to pass down family traditions to or family heirlooms. Including those '80s toys I saved to hopefully show my own child someday. Because doesn't every child want to see toys from the decade when their parents grew up? No? Just me? It's okay, I already know I'm oddly sentimental.

Adoption has been suggested and thought about. And while I would love to do that, purposely becoming a single mother is not something I want to do. I know a lot of kick-butt single moms who have functioned well with the hand they were dealt. But intentionally creating that family dynamic is not currently in my plans. If it were a spouse and me, then adoption might be taken into consideration. In the meantime, I have plenty of little ones around that I can (and do) spoil. It's not abnormal for me to take them on an outing to get ice cream, go bowling, or to the park. You can often find me supporting them at their games and concerts too. That's what honorary aunts do!

Being single used to discourage me, but I've learned to overcome the disappointments and find joy along the way. Through counseling, I've learned that life can still be good without the things I planned at eighteen. It's okay to want them, but I no longer dwell on them and halt my life while waiting for any of them to happen. There's a chance some of it will never happen. And there's a chance that God is using this time to prepare me for when the timing is right. Either way, I have learned to trust God with what He has planned for me. And that's definitely a joyful feeling!

CHAPTER 6

As a single adult, traveling alone is something I have become good at. There was a time when I was watching opportunities pass me by while my list got longer. I had been sitting around and waiting on the right time or the right person to seek adventure with. But once I realized the right time is "now" and that I could seek adventure by myself, I began checking things off my list so quickly that I would frequently get asked, "What's next?"

The desire to check things off my list resulted in me taking solo trips. I was at a point where most of my friends had families of their own, and the people in my life who had time to travel didn't have the money to travel. So, I decided I wasn't going to miss out just because I didn't have travel companions. Would I have rather had others to travel with? Or course. But I didn't want to miss opportunities while waiting for others.

Even though I prefer traveling with others, I have learned that traveling alone can be enjoyable. If I want to listen to the same podcast for 12 hours, then I can do that. If I want to sleep in before I spend the day hiking, then I can do that. Or if I decide I want to get up early to see the sunrise; I can do that too. Wait, get up early? Yeah right. But sign me up for a sunset, and I'll do that in a heartbeat.

Being able to go on a road trip with someone else is a gift to me. I've traveled to some great destinations with others, and the journey of getting there is sometimes the best part. The stories told, the games played, and the funny moments that become inside jokes are some of my favorite things about getting in the car and taking off on an adventure. I'll never forget the time my sister wore a unicorn head in the backseat of the car, waving at everyone while we drove through the streets of downtown Nashville. If you know my sister, then this doesn't surprise you.

These are the kinds of things that embarrass me, and secretly that was her goal. But it was my birthday weekend, and I didn't care. I knew nobody would recognize us, although I still wonder if there is a picture floating around the internet of the crazy lady wearing a unicorn head on Lower Broadway. Another time my friends and I saw a bear cross the road right in front of us. We had just packed up the car to leave the Smoky Mountains, and as we drove away from the condo, Mr. Bear climbed out of the ditch on the passenger side and walked in front of the car. We screamed with excitement as we reached for our cameras, but within seconds he was a memory that only the 3 of us had experienced together. Those are the "you had to be there" moments. And it's the moments I love.

One of my first solo trips was to Yellowstone National Park. After traveling to the park five years earlier with family, I learned snowmobiling tours are available once the park closes for the winter.

I planned a week full of experiences and adventures, beginning with a day of dog sledding in Jackson, WY. Upon arrival, we walked around and met the dogs, a mix of various breeds, including huskies. They all had their own house for shelter from the snow. We were then directed to our sleds, where we met our dog team driver, or musher, Eric, who had moved from Oregon to Wyoming in 2013 and was very passionate about his sled dogs.

One disadvantage of solo travel is being singled out when pairs are created. As I looked around at the other travelers, I was relieved to see another individual among the group. There were four of us on the tour that day, so there was excitement in both of our eyes when we found out we would be paired for one of the sleds. Melanie's bubbly personality made me bond with her instantly.

"Each of you will get a chance to help guide the sled," our musher Eric told us. "Which one of you wants to start in the basket, and who will be driving with me first?" he asked.

After a quick game of rock-paper-scissors, I began the ride in the basket while Melanie stood on the back of the sled with Eric.

We were the lead sled and following closely behind us was the other couple who had the opportunity to drive the sled themselves.

"Hike!" Eric yelled at the dogs so they would start moving.

With a team of eight sled dogs in front of me and the musher behind me doing all of the work, I was tucked in like a burrito in the comfort of the basket as we headed towards Granite Canyon six miles away. The narrow snow-packed trail that led from the kennels to the mountains began to widen into a groomed roadway where we glided through the hills.

There hadn't been a lot of fresh powder lately, so we could hear the snow crunching beneath the sled as 32 dog paws trampled along the path. The sun bounced off the snow and allowed for clear views of the mountains in the distance, which contrasted perfectly against the blue sky.

It wasn't long before I realized how smart the dog team was as they followed commands from the musher when he yelled "Haw!" and "Gee!" to turn left and right.

I quickly noticed how much work the lead dog was doing as the others followed along. "Not every dog can handle the pressure of being the lead dog," Eric explained.

"Ruby is our youngest dog at just over a year old," he told us. "We think Blue is about nine years old."

"At what age do you stop using them?" I heard Melanie ask from the back of the sled.

"On up, Elaina," Eric interrupted. "On up!" The dogs were trying to make a pit stop in the middle of the trail, and I couldn't stop laughing. Trying to run and do their business at the same time. The dogs were the epitome of every runner who knows as soon as you leave the starting line, you inevitably have to use a port-a-potty along the route.

Eric turned his attention back to Melanie's question. "The dogs will let us know when they don't want to pull anymore. For example, they won't come out of their doghouse."

As he told us more about the dog team, I admired the view of Granite Creek, about 200 yards away and about 200 feet down. The water was flowing smoothly between the snow-covered rocks. As the trail continued to twist and turn around the corners, so did the creek, which eventually ran right next to us. But the twists in the path also made it difficult for the dogs to stay on the right side of the trail.

"Gee over. Gee over." Eric commanded them to move to the right.

As I gazed at the mountains in the distance, trying not to look at the eight doggie butts in front of me, I noticed a moose on the hillside to the left. It was antler-free and staring right at us.

"Whoa!" Eric yelled. We stopped long enough to capture a quick picture of the moose. Mr. Moose knew we were there and had his eyes fixed on us, so we quickly got back to sledding before he decided to make his way down the hill toward us.

Halfway into our journey to Granite Canyon, Melanie and I switched places, so I could ride on the back with Eric and help guide Pumpkin, Elaina, Inuit, and the other dogs. As I took my place on the back of the sled and struggled to find a comfortable position for my feet on the inches-wide footboard, I grabbed ahold of the handle just in time for Eric to yell, "Hike!"

Eric taught me how to use the foot break on the back of the sled, which was a claw-like piece of equipment that dug into the snow to slow us down. It was no longer a peaceful and relaxing ride like it was in the basket because I had to balance myself on the footboard while going over bumps and while the dogs weaved through the trail. But it was the adventure I craved and the excitement I needed.

Once we arrived at Granite Canyon, I learned the sled behind us had been carrying supplies for our mid-way stop. Eric and his crew had thought of everything! We unloaded the sleds containing everything we needed for lunch, including thermoses full of hot chili, accompanied by cornbread and all the toppings for chili, and hot water to make hot chocolate. We setup the table in what felt like the middle of nowhere. During our break, we could walk around and take in the snowy white scenery and interact with our dog team while they rested.

After lunch, we packed everything back onto the sleds and switched places for the ride back. The other couple took the lead sled with Eric, and Melanie and I were promoted to mushers as we guided the second sled. We took our positions, looked at each other with questionable confidence, and wondered if we could handle our new jobs of steering, braking, and maneuvering our dogs back to the starting point. Thankfully, sled dogs are very intelligent and will easily follow the lead sled in front of them.

Eric gave us a few instructions before he jumped on the lead sled. "There's one big downhill, so watch the speed and try not to get them in a full gallop because their wrists and shoulders aren't conditioned for it."

Helping guide the dogs was exciting, but it was a lot of work. "This is going to be quite the workout for the next six miles," I joked to Melanie as we tried to keep our balance and keep from falling off.

It was hard to get a glimpse of the scenery and the creek below us while paying attention to upcoming curves so we could slow down for them. The basket ride might have been more relaxing, but being a musher brought out the adventure in me!

Melanie and I learned we had both arrived the day before and had similar plans for the remainder of our trip.

"I have plans to go snowmobiling tomorrow," I told her.

"My husband and I are snowmobiling tomorrow," she said.

"I wonder if we'll see each other. Where are you going?" I asked.

"Yellowstone," she replied.

"I'm doing Yellowstone also, but not until Wednesday, so I guess we won't run into each other. And on Thursday, I will probably go tubing," I told her.

"We are thinking about tubing that day also. We should meet up! I'll text you to let you know our plans," she said excitedly.

Once we arrived back at the kennels, Melanie and I exchanged numbers. We contacted each other just as planned and went tubing together two days later. Bonding with other travelers is one of my favorite things because we have a shared passion and a chance to swap stories and get ideas for new experiences. I wouldn't have met Melanie if I had been traveling with others, which is another advantage of solo traveling.

Days two and three were reserved for snowmobiling. It was the reason I booked the trip, and I woke up early with anticipation when the day had finally arrived. After being picked up in my hotel lobby by the tour company, they drove us back to their store, where they fitted us for our one-piece black and white winter suits. After being supplied with a helmet, we had a lesson on how to drive our snowmobiles. I was happy to know it wasn't much different than operating a 4-wheeler.

Once outside, I found an open snowmobile and got acquainted with the controls we had just learned about. I watched as each person in the group decided who was going to drive the two-seated snowmobiles, and for the first time all week, I was glad I was traveling alone because it meant that I didn't have to share the driving duties and sit on the back…or pay extra to have my own snowmobile.

I climbed onto my snowmobile and started the engine with a bit of a racing heart because I was nervous about keeping up with the group. We were instructed to stay in a single-line formation and not pass each other, so that meant I better not slow down the ones behind me.

Amazing Joy

The National Park had groomed the roadways for snowmobile tours and snow coach tours (the vans with extra-large snow tires), but no other traffic was allowed inside the park during the winter. As we entered Yellowstone National Park, I quickly learned the snowmobile was harder to steer and control than a 4-wheeler because the skis on the front of it would catch in the grooves of the snow just enough to require additional concentration of the trail ahead.

As we rode 45 miles around and witnessed the snowy views of the park, I couldn't help but notice how delightfully pleasing it was to enjoy the peacefulness of being some of the few people inside the park.

Many times throughout the day, we parked our snowmobiles (still in a single line) and got to witness the scenery with frozen lakes in the distance, the snow surrounding the waterfalls, the mud pots bubbling up from the ground, and the main attraction, Old Faithful. We sat on the benches surrounding the mighty geyser and waited for the "next interval" time listed on the sign next to the Visitor Center. It erupted just as predicted and as if it was cued. Watching Old Faithful erupt made me smile because it's astonishing how something in nature can be so predictable for so long. The roar of the boiling water rushing out of the ground for several minutes and the height at which it erupts had me glued to my seat and wishing I could wait for the next eruption to witness it again.

The next day, I began another snowmobile tour, but this time it was through the Togwotee Pass in the Bridger-Teton

National Forest. The adventure was much different than it was through Yellowstone because we rode on trails through the woods. The trails were groomed only by previous snowmobiles, which took more work to control the sleds of the snowmobile in the deep snow. We traveled through the hills instead of on flat roads, we saw views of the Grand Teton Mountain in the distance, and once we reached the open field, we were allowed to turn it loose and create our own path through the even deeper snow. Outside of being an absolute blast, the drawback was being unable to see what was under the snow. After unexpectantly finding a small ditch, I throttled down and casually rode through the field until it was time to head back. Because all I could think about were the repairs I would have to pay for if I damaged something, and that wasn't part of my vacation budget!

I completed the trip with tubing and a lift ride to the top of the ski mountain to overlook the city. The success of the trip gave me the confidence to continue traveling alone. I still travel with others when possible, but if there is somewhere I want to go, then I go. When my choices are to stay home and wait for others to have time off and money to travel or leave for my own adventure and not miss out on a chance to see the world, I have realized I prefer the second choice.

One of my least favorite parts of solo traveling, though, is dining alone. Evidently, the words "table for one" confuses hostesses.

"Just one?" they reply.

"Yes, just one," I confirm.

"Would you like to sit at the bar?" they ask. Because apparently, that's where all the lone diners sit.

So, I tell them, "No, thank you. I would like to sit at a table in the main dining area."

And with a perplexed look on their face, they eventually lead me to a table.

I usually feel very self-conscious when eating alone at a table surrounded by families and couples who are traveling together. Sometimes I try to act busy by going through pictures on my phone to avoid the stares from others. The looks are non-existent, by the way, and only in my head. I quickly re-write the narrative that I'm silently quoting to myself so that I see things from a positive perspective.

Be proud of yourself for having the courage to drive across the country to a place you've never been. You are getting to see things you've never seen before and experience places you might not have the chance to go to again. Look around and take time to notice the family who has had a long day toting around 4 kids. The waiter who is hustling to manage multiple tables yet still has a smile and friendly greeting waiting for you. Or the older lady also sitting by herself who reminds you of your grandmother. Oh, and tell the waitress you will buy the lady's lunch.

Before leaving the small hometown pizza restaurant, I got the attention of the waitress at the table across from me and told her I wanted to pay for the lunch of the lady sitting there.

"That's so sweet of you. Ever since her husband passed away, she comes in regularly to eat lunch," the waitress told me.

As I walked out the door, the waitress informed her customer that I had paid for her meal. At first, I was disappointed she didn't wait until I was gone to tell her because I typically like it to be anonymous when I do that. But when I saw the look of surprise on the face of the woman who was dining alone, it melted my heart. It also reminded me that I would have never felt the joy of making someone else's day if I had been dining with others. I would have been too occupied with mealtime conversations to notice another lone diner. Dining alone is just another way that God gets my attention. My only regret that day was that I didn't notice her sooner and ask to join her. I bet she would have had some great stories to share.

Being a solo traveler is something I wouldn't have seen myself doing 20 years ago, but I have learned to love and find joy in it. It's another reminder to myself that even though things aren't what I had mapped out for my life, there is still so much to be thankful for and look forward to.

CHAPTER 7

March is usually a time of year to enjoy the smells of freshly blooming spring flowers and when the last days of winter start making their exit. But that year, the spring blossoms were the last thing on my mind. March is when my mom started feeling really tired, and not the lack of sleep kind of tired. Although she did wonder at first if that was the reason since she had been working a lot of hours at my dad's office, but she knew it was different and required a trip to the doctor. Her doctor immediately suspected the diagnosis even though there were very few symptoms to gauge it. So, they began running tests to be sure. I was on a plane to Arizona when we heard about the possibility of her diagnosis. I refused to consider what might lie ahead of us and focused on the weekend in the desert's dry heat. I nonchalantly said, "There's no way it's cancer. Not my mom. My mom is going to live forever." The results from her tests came back within a few days. Cancer.

I still didn't believe it. I still kept thinking it was no big deal because people beat cancer every day. So why would she be any different? She was diagnosed with Multiple Myeloma, a rare form of blood cancer, also sometimes referred to as bone cancer since it affects the bone marrow. The prognosis? Treatable, but not curable. Patients have been known to live with it for 10 years, but that's on the good end of the scale. So, while her cancer could not be cured, the doctors felt optimistic about being able to treat it, which would allow her to continue living.

Terminal is a word that should have scared me. But it didn't. I was either in denial or knew in my heart that God would heal her. At the time, I felt like it was my confidence in God's healing. But looking back on it, I'm not sure which one it was.

Chemo treatments began right away at the local hospital. We went into it with a positive attitude from the beginning. Or at least I did; I can't speak for the rest of the family.

Due to it being a rare type of cancer, the local doctors couldn't determine the full treatment plan. Therefore, they scheduled her an appointment with a specialist in St. Louis within a couple of days.

March was the busiest time of year for my dad – tax season – so I agreed to drive Mom to St. Louis for the initial appointment. We were all under the impression that this was to confirm the cancer diagnosis. We soon found out the appointment was to see how bad it was because the doctors already knew it was cancer.

Mom and I sat with hopefulness when the doctor walked into the tiny exam room. The doctor's foreign dialect was difficult to understand at times, and I took notes the best that I could in order to decipher the conversation with the rest of the family when we arrived home.

After an overnight stay in the hotel adjacent to the hospital, I called my dad to update him. "We just finished the bone marrow biopsy and will be headed home shortly."

When friends and family offered to help take her to chemo treatments, we took them up on the offer since we knew this new journey would require a team effort. I was given approved days off from work to help care for her, but since there was a longer hospital stay ahead of us, I knew I would need to use the days when my dad, my sister, and I would take turns staying with her at the hospital for 2-3 weeks.

After a couple of months of chemo, I felt like I wasn't doing my part by sitting beside her while the treatment was administered. And I *wanted* to be there with her. So, I scheduled a day off to drive her to her chemo appointment.

As I sat with her for the first time, I was learning how the process worked. The process she had been doing for months and was a pro at it. "Why have I not been here yet?" I kept thinking. "Why have I been acting like this is no big deal and pretending it's something as simple as a haircut?"

I watched as nurses walked around the room and administered treatment to each patient. "Mom, is that your doctor?" I asked when I realized I didn't even know what her doctor looked like.

"No, you will hear her coming before you see her because she always wears heels that click on the tile as she walks," Mom said with a grin.

When her doctor began approaching, Mom started laughing. The doctor was wearing rubber-soled shoes that day and snuck up on us for the first time since Mom had been seeing her.

In addition to chemo, part of her treatment plan would include a stem cell transplant using her own stem cells. So, to do this, they first had to harvest the stem cells. Then she would undergo an extensive round of chemo to kill all the remaining cells in her body before the harvested ones could be re-implanted. The chemo she received during the stem cell transplant would finally make her beautiful gray hair fall out. She was worried about her hair from the moment of her diagnosis. I would have been worried, too, if it were me. Some women can pull off a bald head, but I know I wouldn't be one of them.

In preparation for the changes in her hair, we took her wig shopping. It was a mixture of fun when laughing at some of the crazy colors and styles she could have gone with, to sadness when watching my mother try on wigs that would hopefully look like her short gray hair with a smidge of curl in it. She wanted a wig the same color and same length as her current hairstyle so that she looked like herself and as normal as possible. It was a hard process to go through, but in a way, it was just another step in the journey.

Throughout every step, whether it was in the plan or a setback, I just kept asking, "Now what"? As in, "Okay, that treatment didn't work. Now what?" or "She has a new symptom that needs to be treated. Now what?" It never crossed my mind that the setbacks would be roadblocks we couldn't get past. So, I kept following the plan. Just going through the motions instead of the emotions. It's hard to stop and process the emotional side of things when all of your focus is on the positive side. I'm not saying there is a positive side to having cancer, but I was trying to have a positive attitude through it and believe that she would beat it.

Her stem cell transplant went as planned, and her recovery went better than planned. She had to stay in the hospital until her white blood cell count reached a certain level which was estimated to take two weeks. About a week after her transplant, her numbers looked great, so the doctors let her go home. That was my week to stay with her in St. Louis, so I had the honor of driving her home, where family members and friends greeted her with a surprise welcome home. They were waiting for her in the front yard as we pulled into the driveway.

As she settled in with her new wig, she was feeling better for probably the first time since her diagnosis six months earlier. We were so excited that the treatment worked.

Mom began getting her strength back and started to seem like herself again. Her smile was back, and it felt good to see her moving around without pain.

That fall, I remember telling her I planned to see the Rockefeller Christmas tree in New York City in December. It was on my ever-growing bucket list, so I was ready to check it off.

I noticed Mom's ears perked up when I told her. So, I decided to ask. "Mom, do you want to go with me?"

I was shocked by her answer and elated when she said yes. We decided to make it a family vacation, and as a family of four, my mom, dad, sister, and I boarded a plane to NYC the first weekend in December. We had been to NYC once before, but this was a new experience to be there during the winter. My sister and I told our parents to enjoy dinner by themselves on the first night to celebrate their wedding anniversary. Afterward, the four of us walked around to look at decorations that had been placed around the city.

We did all the Christmas-y things, which included Rockefeller Center to see the Christmas tree and watch the ice skaters, a bus ride on the top of a double-decker bus to see the city's Christmas lights (yes, it was cold), tickets to see the Rockettes perform at Radio City Music Hall, and we even ate chestnuts by an open fire. Well, technically, they were from a hot dog stand in Times Square, but we did eat chestnuts.

New York City involves a LOT of walking. On a map, the distance between destinations seems much shorter and gave us encouragement to walk. We didn't see the need to pay for a taxi when we could walk there. "It's just a few blocks," we would say to each other. But those "blocks" were not like the ones we had back home. They extend further in NYC and become 2-3 of the blocks we were used to. So, we began taking the subway even when it seemed like a short distance. But taking the subway still provided challenges because there are stairs to walk down to the platform, sometimes multiple flights, and depending on which train you need, there might be additional walking to get on the train. And finally, there are more stairs to climb when exiting the subway terminal.

So, while Mom felt good after her transplant, this trip wore her out very quickly. She was exhausted and chose to miss a few outings to get some rest.

"Go without me today," she told us one afternoon.

I hated seeing her that way and not being able to enjoy the trip fully. We created a lot of great memories, though. Seeing Mom's smile while watching the Rockettes perform was a gift. That trip was one of my favorites and saddest at the same time because it ended up being our last one together.

As the new year rolled around, Mom began to feel tired again. At first, we thought it was because she had been working again and wasn't used to the long hours. But it didn't take long to realize it was more than that. Her cancer was already coming back.

So, just like it was with all the other news we had been given, I was thinking, "Okay, no big deal, she'll have more treatments and be fine." It began a series of hurdle after hurdle, but I still never took the time to think she wasn't going to push through each one. One of the major hurdles was when she was having very sharp headaches. We found out she had a brain bleed due to her platelets being too low. So, the doctors addressed that. It should have been a clue to me that she wasn't doing good, and I hate that I never realized she wasn't going to beat this.

She had pneumonia at one point and was in the hospital for that. She had issues inside her mouth, which we later discovered were caused by the cancer. She lost her balance and fell a few times, so we thought it might have been another brain bleed. But when we got the results of the scans back that time, we were told the effects of the cancer had reached her head. She had lesions on the outside of her skull, but there was also one inside her skull that was starting to penetrate the lining of the brain. Another setback.

Because of the new symptoms, the doctors recommended that she begin radiation since the chemo wouldn't penetrate the skull. We began seeing side effects of the radiation, which were causing her to lose her balance even more and be very confused. But again, I just kept thinking, "We have to get her through the radiation treatments, and then she'll be like herself again."

All that time, I should have asked my mom about her emotions and what she was thinking and feeling. I should have even had the conversation about whether or not she was afraid to die. But I was still in denial and didn't think that conversation needed to happen because I thought she would pull through. It was also very hard for me to have serious conversations, so it was easier not to attempt it.

I struggle with telling people how I feel, and it's even hard for me to listen to how they feel. But I wish so badly that I had asked her. Asked her what it felt like. Asked her if it hurt. Asked her if she was sad. Asked her if she was scared.

Anything but the silence I gave when we were alone or the jokes I would tell to try to make her feel better. It was hard to witness the pain she was in, and I know a lot of that pain was heartache because I wouldn't talk to her. It wasn't just her illness that I couldn't talk about, though. I hardly ever had a serious conversation with my mom (or anyone else) because the thought of it made my heart race to the point of almost having a panic attack. So instead, I just kept all of my thoughts bottled up inside. And it's a regret that I continue to have.

CHAPTER 8

It was a Thursday, and I was at my desk on the 3rd floor of the technology building when I found out.

"They are going to stop treatment," the text said.

"Stop treatment?" What did that mean? Are they going to stop this one and find a new one? I don't understand. Stop it for good? I had so many questions.

I had seen my mom four days earlier and didn't think she was as bad as the text was making it sound. With my phone and keys in hand, I walked towards the back set of stairs to prevent anyone from seeing the tears welling up in my eyes. I proceeded downstairs to the first floor and across the parking lot where my car sat. I made a phone call to clarify the text and found out the doctors were basically saying that the chemo was just making her worse at this point.

I sat in my car to process what I had just heard, pulled myself together, and walked back upstairs to my desk. As I sat in front of my computer screen, surrounded by the blue cubicle walls, I hoped nobody would approach my desk because the emotions hadn't left entirely yet. Within a few minutes, I knew I wouldn't be able to sit there for seven more hours, so I sent my manager a note and said I was going home "sick."

In the meantime, Mom was transferred to the hospital to run additional tests before the doctors made their conclusion. I resumed communication with the family once I got home, but I still wasn't understanding the message of how bad things were. In the past month, we had made multiple trips to the hospital and ER, and each time we were sent home with a new plan or new medicine. In my mind, I still thought this was another one of those instances.

Within an hour, I got a phone call that said, "You need to be here."

As I packed my car, my friends waited in the driveway while insisting on driving me to Missouri. I was aware that I would be more emotional if I weren't the one deciding the speed and route to take, so I finally agreed for one of them to ride with me and one to follow me.

Halfway to the hospital, I received another phone call. "Where are you? How close are you?" my aunt asked.

"I'm about 30 minutes away," I told her.

"Ok, good, your mom is asking where you are," she replied.

I lost it. The tears immediately began streaming down my face as I tried to focus on the road. First, I couldn't believe it took me so long to get in the car and drive to the hospital, and I was mad at myself for that. Second, I hated that my mom had to ask about me because it took me so long to get there, and I wasn't in the room with the rest of the family. These two things still bother me today. The guilt began to overtake my sadness, and it felt like the next 30 minutes lasted three hours.

When I arrived at the hospital, the hallway was full of family members. Her siblings, her father, her in-laws, my dad's siblings – it felt like everyone was there BUT ME. "Why did I wait so long to go there?" I kept asking myself. Seeing everyone who had arrived before me felt like a gut punch, and I felt like they were looking at me with disappointment because I was one of the last ones to get there. It was so unlike me to not be right there when something happened, but I truly didn't understand the severity of our new setback.

As I walked in, her eyes shifted toward the door, and even though she didn't smile or greet me in any way, I could see the relief in her eyes. I couldn't believe how different she looked from the last time I saw her, four days before. It finally hit me that she was worried I wouldn't make it in time to say goodbye.

My aunt pulled me aside in the hall and told me, "You need to say your goodbyes now, just in case she goes into an unconscious state sooner rather than later."

I stared at the floor in disbelief but knew she was right. The ones who had arrived before me had already had their one-on-one time inside Mom's tiny hospital room, and now it was my turn. I walked back into her room, kissed her forehead, and sat in the cold plastic chair beside her bed.

And then silence. The words weren't there, and even if they were, they wouldn't have made it past the lump in my throat. I sat in silence while trying to comprehend the stage we were in.

As evening approached, we discussed who would stay at the hospital that night and who would go home and try to rest since we knew we had some long days ahead of us.

I left the hospital that evening and drove to my parent's house. As I lay in bed inside the walls of my childhood bedroom that night trying to sleep, the thoughts racing through my mind prevented me from getting any rest. Morning arrived quickly, and the eerie sounds of my alarm reminded me that our appointment with the doctor was looming.

The family gathered in mom's hospital room and awaited the doctor's return when she would tell us the results of the latest tests. We were almost sure we knew the outcome and what she would say. And it was the words we feared.

We heard the click-clack of the doctor's heels coming down the hall. "There's nothing else we can do," she told us. "She only has a few days to a few weeks left, so I recommend you take her home for hospice care and make her as comfortable as possible."

And now, suddenly, I was begging for that 10-year prognosis we were given at the beginning of her illness.

Since we didn't know how long she would hold on, I told my boss I wouldn't be back to work as long as she was still with us. There was no way I was going to leave her side now.

The narrow hallway outside Mom's room continued to be crowded with family as each of us trickled in and out. The hospital staff recognized the number of family members who weren't planning to leave and generously found a larger room to move her to that night. A few of us stayed all night at the hospital with her to make sure she wasn't alone. We sat on the bench in the corner of the room, telling stories and watching her vitals. As evening approached, her eyes struggled to stay open, and we all knew she was tired. Tired from lack of sleep and most likely tired of fighting the nasty disease she had been plagued with. I also feel like she was afraid to close her eyes because she knew it might be the last time to look at us.

I still had not been able to tell my mom goodbye. I had tried a few times, but I couldn't. And now I was getting distraught that I would miss my chance to tell her while she was still awake and able to comprehend what I was saying. I asked my sister to help me, and we devised a plan for me to write everything I wanted to say, and then I could read it to Mom. Words seem to come easier when I'm writing them. So that's what I did. I found a small quiet room down the hall and opened my laptop. There were so many things I should have said over the years, and now I was trying to reduce it to a couple of short paragraphs. I struggled with finding the right words to convey my message and squeeze in all the feelings I had never shared.

Once I was ready, my sister asked everyone to leave the room. I was so nervous. "Why was I nervous as I walked into the room to talk to my mom?" I thought to myself. I crawled onto the side of her bed where the rail had been lowered, and with my laptop in hand, I tried reading the words to her. Even though I had the words written, they still wouldn't come out of my mouth. After a few minutes, I was finally able to tell her the things I needed to, including that I was sorry for not having serious conversations with her. She always thought it was only her I didn't talk to. So, I tried to explain that it wasn't just her and that I struggled with opening up and telling people how I felt. In her mumbled voice, it took a lot of physical strength for her to say, "I know." I felt a little bit of relief knowing she understood my struggle with communication. But I was also kicking myself for never addressing it before that moment because now I'll never be able to have a true heart-to-heart conversation with my mom.

The next morning, we decided to take Mom home for hospice care. She was not able to ride home in a car, so we opted to have medical transport take her home. As I left the hospital parking lot that day, I ended up right behind the ambulance that my mom was in. And every time we stopped at a traffic light, I could see her through the back window. Tears flowed down my cheeks every time because it hit me that we were taking her home to die.

It was now Saturday afternoon, and we tried to make her comfortable in the hospital bed, which was placed in the living room next to her favorite window. We thought she would enjoy looking out and seeing her beautiful flowers in the garden. We also played Christmas music throughout the afternoon because it was her favorite. The smell of roasted peanuts lingered in the air from the kitchen because we knew it was another thing she loved. Since I hadn't slept much the last two days, I took a quick nap on the couch. The noise drifting from the kitchen and living room didn't bother me because I was just like everyone else and didn't want to stray too far from Mom's side. After a short rest, I realized Mom hadn't woken up in a while, and that's when it hit me that she had fallen into the unconscious state, which we had been told would be next. And now it was obvious that the "days to weeks" prediction from the doctor was going to be "days."

As evening approached, my dad, my sister, my mom's sisters, and I all gathered around her bedside and prepared ourselves to sit by her side through the night. Each of us held her hands to let her know we were there and did everything we could to make sure she was comfortable. Mom gave us a few scares throughout the night when we thought she had stopped breathing. She held on until Sunday morning when the rest of her siblings and her father arrived as we all crowded together in the living room.

There was still a chance she would hold on for several more days. We had been keeping a close eye on her body temperature, and by early afternoon we noticed it began to drop as her blood circulation slowed down.

And as we sat around her bedside on Sunday afternoon, we watched her take her last breath. I was holding her hand when she breathed for the last time, and as I looked at her hand in mine, I literally watched the blood stop flowing through her body. It started in her fingertips and moved up her arm. Pale white. That's the color her hand was now that the blood wasn't flowing through it.

We cried together as a family and sat with her until the coroner arrived. And then we watched as her body was loaded into the coroner's car and left the driveway. That's the moment I completely lost it. The moment when it finally hit me that she was gone. A lot of things changed in that moment. That exact moment. But the love she showed me for 34 years is something I'll remember forever. I was already counting all of the ways I was going to miss her.

That night, I sat on the edge of my bed and stared at the wall in disbelief.

"She wasn't supposed to die! Why did God let her die?!" is all I could think.

The clarinet squeaks during fifth-grade band that came from the same room I was now weeping in were no match for the screams I wanted to let out. I wanted to punch things, slam things, and use a baseball bat to hit anything I could find. The rage inside of me never escaped and remained bottled up like every other emotion I ever felt.

As I went to bed that night, I was still in shock. I was the saddest I had ever been. I regretted all the things I never told my mom. I was hurting for my mom because I knew she wanted to live longer. And I was mad that she was taken from us so early.

I was exhausted from not sleeping the last few nights and drained from the rollercoaster of emotions we just went through and the thought of the ones we still had ahead of us. As I lay there trying to fall asleep, my entire body began to tremble. From head to toe shaking uncontrollably. I guess the emotions I had been trying so hard to ignore were now busting their way out.

When I woke up the next morning, I wanted to hear her walking down the hall, but instead, it was the realization that she'd never walk past my bedroom door again.

The next few days, we just went through the motions. Planning. Visitation. Funeral.

As the last note of "Amazing Grace" played at Mom's funeral service, the stark reality of her absence set in. In the days after her death, we told stories and celebrated her life and the good times we shared.

In the weeks after her death, the anguish of depression set in. It was like being hit by a car. Which is another thing I had to endure just days after my mom's funeral. Getting hit by a car, that is.

At the 4-way stop of our small one-light town is where the man in the green SUV plowed down my dad and me as we crossed the street. "Please don't take another parent from me," I thought as we both fell to the ground in the middle of Main Street. Thankfully it was a rolling impact instead of a sudden one, and we both walked away with only soreness and a scare.

My mom's illness and death were also a rolling impact. I saw it coming just like I saw the SUV come to a complete stop and then accelerate as we began to cross the street. Maybe if I had yelled at God the same way I yelled "STOP!" at the SUV driver while beating on the hood of his car, then He would have healed my mom. Did I not beg enough? Did I not pray enough? I thought prayer was supposed to heal people. It heals other people, so why didn't it heal my mom?

So many questions that I didn't know how to process.

Some things began to change immediately, like my mom not being there to walk me to my car on Sunday nights with a bowl of leftovers, which had been our routine for over 10 years. And she wouldn't be waiting for my "I'm home," text once I arrived back in Arkansas.

Another immediate change was our family dynamic. In a blink of an eye and her last breath, we went from four to three. My place in the family was changing, and I wondered how long we would stay as three. I realized I had to prepare myself for a chance of it going back to four or greater. I had always been the youngest of the family, but what if I suddenly became the middle child? What if I gained step-sisters? It could either take away from the only dynamic I ever knew or add to it. And there was no way of knowing which one it would be if that situation arose, so the unknown created fear in me.

I overthought all of it and played out different scenarios in my head. I didn't like any of them. I wanted things to stay the way they always were. Except that things did change because Mom was gone now. And I didn't handle it well. I acted like a child. A child who doesn't know how to process their feelings. Or a 34-year-old child who never learned how to either.

And what about the only home I had until I was 22? Would the only house I ever knew as home be gone? The place I learned how to walk and the place where I played kickball in the hallway while my parents had card night in the kitchen. The same hallway where I could hear my mom giggling from the other end when she found the foil on April Fool's Day. The home where I crashed my bike outside and got my first set of stitches. The home where I saved the Princess for Mario for the first time. The one where I cried on the kitchen floor because my first boyfriend moved away, and my mom begged me to tell her what was wrong. The one where the first "everythings" happened, and the last breath my mom took happened. I know that change will happen, and someday that house will belong to another family. But I can only process one change at a time and couldn't think about the what-ifs.

I wish I could say my last tear fell simultaneously with the last leaf of fall. But alas, that's when all of the "firsts" began. After losing a loved one, the "firsts" are those events where they should have been.

The first birthday, first holiday, first wedding anniversary, first time eating at their favorite restaurant without them, and the first vacation without them. When Mom's next birthday arrived, we tried our best to celebrate it with good memories as we gobbled down her favorite cheddar biscuits.

As Christmas began to roll around, I knew it wouldn't be easy since she was the type to go all-out when decorating. She had a specific spot for everything and remembered where each figurine went every year. She would even take down pictures on the wall to put up Christmas wreaths, clocks, etc.

Since I typically had the Friday after Thanksgiving off from work, I helped Mom put up the Christmas decorations each year. And the first year she wasn't there to place everything where it went, I decided I was going to attempt to make it look like she did. I carried box after box upstairs from the basement and began taking inventory. But the emotions quickly took over, and I couldn't continue any further. I called my aunt to help me, and together the two of us worked our magic. We placed the village houses on top of the TV, stockings on the bookcase, and pillows on the couch, decorated the tree, assembled her Santa collection above the kitchen cabinets, and then made our best guesses at where the rest of it went.

It took us several hours to complete, but I enjoyed looking at Mom's favorite items. She definitely loved Christmas and put a lot of effort into making it look festive. I can't say the same for myself, though, because that year was the only time all the boxes of decorations were emptied. That was too much work for me!

My own birthday was another difficult holiday when I realized the woman who gave birth to me wasn't there to celebrate with me. And Valentine's Day was ironically hard as well because it was another way she showed us her love by making sure we all had a card, candy, and a small present each year.

Each "first" brought on a new set of emotions, and when we made it to the one-year anniversary of her passing away, we gathered as a family to acknowledge her memory.

"But now what? How do we handle each of these milestones going forward?" I remember thinking.

They are no longer "firsts," and the realization of her being gone had fully set in. That's when the grief really kicked in for me.

Grief is different for everyone. And I have witnessed how true it is that each person handles grief differently. I went through each stage of grief, and I can also confirm there is no set amount of time for going through each stage.

My denial started long before my mom passed away. During her illness, I was in denial that she might not survive. I knew in my heart that she would pull through and be here for many more years. So, I quickly moved to the anger stage when she passed away. I was angry about everything. And I was especially angry at God for allowing this to happen.

The first moments of grief are like being in a dunk tank. You're casually sitting on the bench above the water, knowing that someone will eventually hit the bullseye. You can see it coming, and you think you're ready. But then suddenly, you're under four feet of water. The water is shallow enough to stand up, so you get up and climb back on the bench, only to be thrust into the water again when the next ball is thrown. I climbed back on the bench too many times before realizing the only way to stop falling in the water was to get out of the tank. And that meant I had to seek help to get me out of the cycle of the dunk tank.

Unfortunately, I went through the initial stages of grief alone and didn't seek help until I was a few years into it. I had hit the depression stage of grief by the time I realized I needed the guidance of a professional. I was lucky to find an amazing counselor who helped me reach the last stage of grief by finding acceptance. She helped me to have hope again.

I now see life from a whole different view because of the counseling I've gone through. Counseling that I would have never gone to if it weren't for the grief of losing a loved one. So, while my mom dying didn't bring joy, my perspective on life DID change because she died. Losing her was a harsh reminder of how short life really is. I used to plan to do things "when I retire" instead of living in the now. I used to think "someday" was something we could all look forward to, but what if we leave this earth before our "someday" arrives? We have to live every day as if it is our "someday," and that's exactly what I changed in my life due to the grief that I went through.

You've probably heard many times that you should spend more time with family. I'm grateful for the years spent with my mom, and the weekends I went home to visit. I also find gratefulness in being single because I don't think I would have been able to spend as much time with my mom before and during her illness if I had my own family to care for. So regardless of what age you are, go visit your parents. Do whatever it takes to stay in touch with them.

Amazing Joy

I was 34 years old when my mom passed away. I would have never imagined I would be without a mom at that age. Losing her changed a lot of things and changed my outlook on life. I had always joked about the saying "life is short," but after losing a loved one, that saying becomes so much more real.

It's strange to think something as hurtful as grief can lead to something happy. Although it's not the event itself that led to joy, but rather my reaction to it and how I chose to live afterward.

CHAPTER 9

In the past, I was someone who kept my emotions, feelings, and words bottled up inside. The walls I used to put up were my comfort zone. And when I say walls, I'm talking about the Great-Wall-of-China-nobody-is-getting-past-them kind of walls. It started as a child and was most likely caused by the fear that someone would laugh at me. Cue the social anxiety.

I had known for a long time that I should get help to address my inability to open up, but again the anxiety affected that too. The thought of being in a room with only one other person and being required to talk to them made me more nervous than coming face to face with a 13,000-pound elephant on an African safari.

On the rare occasion when I would open up to someone, it was typically not in a public location due to the fear of someone overhearing me. AND, if on the even rarer occasion that I have a serious conversation in public, you might notice that I strategically sit with my back to a wall so that I can see everyone and not be worried that someone will walk up behind me and hear the conversation. This is where I admit I'm full of issues.

Several years ago, I was in a place where I was unhappy with a lot of things and basically life in general. I wasn't happy at work, I wasn't happy in my relationships, and I saw no change in the near future for either one of them. And then the depression came barreling in like an unwelcomed guest through the front door. I knew it was happening but was too scared to ask for help. And probably afraid of what people would think when they found out. So, I kept it to myself and did what I could to fight it. Sometimes that meant going out to dinner with friends to take my mind off things, and other times it meant going on a road trip to get out of the house.

As the heartaches continued to pile up, my emotions were given another battle to fight when I was faced with the loss of a loved one. I didn't think I would have to manage that for another thirty years. I wasn't prepared for it and didn't think it would hit me as hard as it did. But when my mom passed away, my emotions spiraled even worse. Denial, anger, depression…you name it, and I was feeling it. But I still tried to ignore it while pretending I was okay. On the outside, I probably looked fine. Those who were close to me knew otherwise. My family encouraged me to seek help, and even though I knew they were right, I couldn't do it because of the anxiety I felt anytime I considered talking to someone.

I'm thankful for the friend who never gave up on me. She could have walked away many times, especially when I took my emotions out on her, but she stuck with me. She saw me in the dark place where I was questioning my beliefs and became the encouragement I needed to turn things around. She wasn't the first to suggest counseling, but I knew she was right and that I needed a professional to walk me through the struggles of grief. She gave me the support I needed to take that step and finally convinced me to see a counselor. I knew in my heart all along that I needed to go, so after our Friday morning breakfast at the donut shop, I promised her I would look into it.

That night, I sat in front of my laptop, staring at a blank Google page. I made it more difficult than it needed to be when I struggled with the right words to search for. Deep down, I feared getting the results from my search because it meant I had to take the next action. Another thing about my anxiety is that I hate making phone calls. So, when the search results came back, I knew I wouldn't be able to pick up the phone to make an appointment. I'd rather run 30 miles and do 100 split-squats than make a phone call. I was relieved when the search results showed someone with an online form for requesting appointments. Upon that discovery, I didn't hesitate to fill it out. Just kidding, I still hesitated!

The reply to set up my first appointment made me nervous, but it was also comforting to know I was finally brave enough to consider talking to a counselor. Yes, I said "consider" it. I still hadn't committed to anything at this point, so you can probably imagine the pat on the back that I gave myself when I finally showed up at her office.

My appointment day arrived. I thought making the appointment was difficult, but I soon realized that was the easy part. As I pulled into the parking lot on the morning of my first appointment, I wanted to turn around and leave. When I got to the door, I still wanted to walk back to my car and leave. Once I made it inside and into the room for my session, not only did I want to leave, but I also wanted to vomit! That would have left a lasting impression!

Before I began going to counseling and therapy, all I knew was what I had seen on TV. Sitcoms and movies are really good at poking fun at therapy sessions, which usually begin with the client (or patient, or whatever we are called) lying on the couch. And then they proceed to spill their guts, and we hear the laugh-track in the background. I kept thinking about this all the way to my appointment, and as I walked up the stairs and stepped through the doorway. When we headed to the room where my session would take place, there it was. THE COUCH. I glanced left, then right, and then darted for the chair in the corner. I couldn't bring myself to sit on the couch because I thought it would make me feel like I was the punchline of the joke I knew from TV. And to this day, I still haven't sat on the couch.

Inside those concrete walls, which put me at ease since I was confident nobody could hear us, I began to tell my story. NOT! That's what was supposed to happen, but instead, my counselor had to drag it out of me one... question… at… a… time. I was so uncomfortable that I imagine my face was the color of every t-shirt in Razorback stadium on a Saturday in October, and I couldn't wait for my 50 minutes to be over.

Getting the first session out of the way took a lot of weight off my shoulders, but I knew I'd have to return before seeing any results. So far, it had taken a lot of courage to research counselors, make the appointment, drive there, walk in the door, and sit down in the room. Every one of those things was outside of my comfort zone. But the courage didn't end there. Once the session was over, I had enough courage to schedule the next appointment, and then the next, and the next one after that. Each session started to get a little easier. Well, until the homework assignments started rolling in. That challenged my courage in a completely different way.

It took MANY counseling sessions for me to get where I am today, and I'm forever grateful to my counselor for being patient with me and encouraging me the entire time. She is supportive, pushes me outside my comfort zone, and is my sounding board when I need someone to run things by. She challenges me in ways that make me look forward to the next homework assignment. (But shhhh, don't tell her that. Let's just keep that part between you and me!) It's an exciting feeling whenever I have completed one of those assignments since most of them are things I never thought I could accomplish. And just like a kid in school, I like to return the following session and get my (imaginary) gold star for completing the assignment.

Some of those assignments have included trying new things to expand my network, getting involved in new groups and making new connections, taking risks, eliminating toxic people from my life, being more vulnerable by sharing my feelings, better communication, joining a new church, and finding joy in the little things. Before counseling, my comfort zone was very small. And through these assignments, my comfort zone has been expanded to where certain situations don't seem impossible anymore. I'm now less anxious when one of these situations comes up. The skills I have learned for managing various circumstances are invaluable to me and have made every hour of counseling worth it.

I recall one assignment where I was supposed to make a list throughout the week. I entered the room, handed her my homework assignment, and headed toward my chair. As she began to read it, she paused and said, "Well, this is interesting," about one of the items.

"That's four words I never want to hear my counselor say," I responded with a grin.

Then we both laughed about it.

Laughing is something I often do in counseling. If there is a rule about only being serious in a counseling session, I'm breaking it because, apparently, I can't be serious for an entire hour. Sometimes I use laughter as a way to deal with pain, so I make jokes to avoid the hurt. I feel like if I laugh about it, then I don't have to address the true emotion tied to it. It's my coping mechanism. I guess we know what I'm talking about in counseling next week!

But when I'm not trying to suppress my emotions with humor, then it's just me trying to make a joke and be a bright spot in someone's day. Like the time I applauded her for the quick math she did in her head. "Wow, that was impressive," I jokingly told her. "Now YOU get a gold star."

I'm sure I can't be the only one who has tried to make their counselor laugh, so let's see a show of hands!

One of the first things we worked on was gratitude. The first week's journaling assignment was to document 3 highs for the day as well as 3 lows. The lows weren't part of the gratitude exercise, but to give my counselor an insight into my feelings since she quickly figured out I wouldn't be talking about my feelings.

After a few weeks of this, the journaling turned into only documenting the highs each day. This might have included leaving work on time, not having to deal with an upset customer that day, going to lunch with friends, or watching a new episode of my favorite show. As you can see, none of my highs for the day were anything extraordinary, like winning the lottery.

This exercise eventually turned into me being able to see joy in all the little things since the key was to look at all the positive things which happened in my day instead of focusing on the negative things. Similar to seeing the glass half full versus half empty. At first, it wasn't easy because I only wanted to think about the things which had upset me that day or made me mad. If someone had cut me off in traffic on the way to work, that stuck with me the rest of the day. But through the steps I took in counseling, I was learning to look at the positive side of things which eventually overtook the negative.

Did frustrating things still happen? Of course, they did. In the same way that positive things were always happening, but I refused to acknowledge them. It's been said that the things you focus on will be the things that control you. And I can attest to that!

I have a feeling you may think I'm crazy for suggesting you can have joy even on a bad day. So, let me give you a better example. I recently ordered takeout because, well, that's what I like to do. I drove to pick it up and got all the way home before I realized they had forgotten my side of brussels sprouts. And my MAIN reason for picking this restaurant was because I was craving the brussels sprouts. So, I'm sure you can imagine my frustration. I called the restaurant, and they said I could either have a gift card for next time or they would have the brussels sprouts ready when I got there if I wanted to drive back. I didn't want to drive back…but I wanted my brussels sprouts, so I got in the car and headed back.

But can we pause for a second and acknowledge the fact that I NEVER thought I'd be saying I was craving brussels sprouts, nor that I was making a special trip for them?

Ok, back to the story. As I was driving back to the restaurant, which was a 15-minute drive each way, I noticed the sunset. The gorgeous multi-colored sunset full of pinks and oranges that was beginning to happen on my previous drive home, and now I was getting to enjoy it a second time. The drive I wouldn't have had if the restaurant hadn't forgotten my side of brussels sprouts. The frustration of making a second trip was gone, and now the additional drive was worth it. Oh, and did I mention they gave me a free dessert also? But that's not the point.

Yes, this example is silly, and there are many hard things in life that seem so bad and so negative that there is no way they could be turned into a positive. Like maybe a job termination which your mortgage depends on, a cancer diagnosis, a car wreck that causes life-altering injuries, a stroke that paralyzes you, or the loss of a loved one. But maybe because of one of these things, you now have the chance to show your faith to someone. Or you might be led to an even better job which you would have never looked for if you hadn't been terminated.

I understand it's hard to see the positive in things when you are hurting or when your world is turned upside down. I'm definitely not here to tell you it's easy. But I am here to tell you it's worth it. Because my life was turned upside down whenever my mom passed away, and I've been able to find joy in everyday life.

Think about what happened in your day today. Now, pick one negative thing that happened. I'm sure there are many to choose from but just pick one. Go ahead; I'll wait. And now, while considering that negative thing, think about one good thing that happened because of it. You may not believe there is anything positive about it, but I'm sure there is. Were you late to work because you were stuck in traffic? If so, I bet you got to listen to your favorite radio station or podcast a little longer while sitting in traffic. That sounds like joy to me! Was the drive-through lane slower than usual? If so, maybe you got more time in the car with your kids before dropping them off at school. Did someone cut in line in front of you at the grocery store? Now that you had to wait longer, you remembered the bread and had time to grab it before you left the store instead of making a second trip. That really sounds like joy to me!

In addition to choosing joy, counseling has created an overall mind shift in me by teaching me to look at things from different angles. When it came to big decisions, like career moves, I always looked for permanent solutions instead of living in the moment and seeing what could happen. Maybe it will work, and maybe it won't. This is why my counselor likes to ask me, "What's the worst that can happen?" The first time she asked me this, my mind went to the most basic answer. For example, "I could fail." Only to be asked the follow-up question, "Okay, what's the worst that can happen if you fail?" We followed the trail of answers until we genuinely got to the worst thing that could happen. And it turns out, the worst wasn't as bad as I thought it would be. Don't get me wrong, it could have been bad emotionally and mentally, but the overall situation wasn't something I couldn't recover from. So, I agreed to start taking small risks. Baby steps.

When it came to taking risks, I had always feared the end result. "What if I make the wrong decision?" is the question that was always on my mind. I would also try to figure out every step and every result before jumping into something. But I learned I don't have to have it all figured out before doing it. When I was trying to find a new job, I kept saying, "But what if I don't like it after a few years?"

And I learned the answer was "then you find something else."

I'm not typically a risk-taker. But I've taken some significant risks over the past few years because I have learned I will never grow in life if I don't try. I would remain stuck in the same place year after year and always wondering what would have happened if I had just tried __________.

Attending counseling sessions quickly became easy for me because of the person sitting across from me. Finding a counselor is simple. But finding the right counselor is difficult. Or so I've heard. Each counselor is different, and sometimes the process requires switching counselors multiple times before finding the right one. I have often said how lucky I am that my search led me to an amazing counselor who was a great fit for me because she made me feel comfortable enough to return for additional sessions.

Her caring demeanor and compassionate personality are exactly what I needed. She shares my love of travel, participates in my humorous banter, and appreciates my quirkiness in wearing colored sneakers.

"I'm amazed at how your sneakers always match your clothes perfectly," she frequently tells me.

And, of course, it's now a joke for me to pick the perfect pair of shoes for my next session. And yes, they will match my outfit!

Counseling has been a game-changer for me. It has helped me push myself to do things I couldn't do in the past, like walk into a room full of strangers and join their class. Or take a risk and quit my passionless job to find something better. But one of the biggest things it has helped me with is my communication. Now I can be more open and share what I'm thinking and feeling. I'm able to have real discussions with people instead of just talking about the weather. I've always been a good listener, but now I try to be an equal participant in conversations.

None of these things would have been possible without the work I've put in with my counseling sessions. I didn't just go to counseling. I kept going to counseling. And kept going. And kept putting in the work. Because I knew nothing was going to change if I didn't put in the work. Putting in the work sometimes means obeying God even when we don't understand.

Counseling is a huge part of my journey because, without it, I would still be stuck in the same cycle of waking up each day and going through the motions to survive the day. If only I could go back and start my counseling journey as a teenager so that I knew how to handle "life" through the years.

Before counseling, life's curve balls used to knock me down. As a former softball catcher, I remember when I was the one calling the pitches. If I called for a curveball, I knew to be prepared for it. But what if I wasn't calling the pitches and I was expecting a change-up, only to be surprised by a fastball? Life tends to be the same way sometimes. I have learned over the years that I'm okay with change as long as I'm the one initiating it or I'm prepared for it. But if something unexpected happens and catches me off guard, I don't handle it well. Life is always going to throw us curve balls. But it's how we choose to handle them that makes the difference. Through counseling, I now have the tools and am better equipped to manage life's curveballs.

I have been in a good place for a few years now, but I still have regular check-ins with my counselor for two reasons. 1) I want to STAY in a good place and not fall back into depression. 2) She helps me with so much more than I could have imagined, like life's big decisions. For someone who is single, I don't often have that one person I can go to for advice and support. So, my counselor is that person for me, and I can count on her to tell me like it is and have my back at the same time. She's someone I can bounce ideas off of and someone who will help me see all sides when making decisions. She won't MAKE the decisions for me but does help me to see all the options. Although sometimes I think it would be easier if she DID decide for me. Oh wait, then I wouldn't be growing and pushing myself.

My life has been transformed over the last few years. Growth has come out of tragedy, and the growth is revealing a person that had been lost. Through counseling, I went from being someone who questioned everything about her life, including her spiritual beliefs, to someone who found a new church home, regularly serves at church, is thriving in a new career, someone who chooses joy, and is living out her dreams.

Even though I started going to counseling for grief, I soon discovered it would help in other areas of my life, also. I would soon learn that it was one of my best decisions.

I used to be someone who didn't think I needed counseling and was embarrassed about going. But now, I'm a believer in what it can do to help our lives, and I recommend it every time I get the opportunity. I believe our mental health should be taken as seriously as our physical health. And having seen the benefits of counseling first-hand, I'm hoping to help normalize it so that others will be encouraged to go.

Now, if you'll excuse me, I have to go collect my gold star for being vulnerable enough to share my story with you!

CHAPTER 10

Being raised in a Christian home is one of the many things I am thankful for. Getting up and going to church every Sunday might not have always been something I looked forward to, but looking back on it now, I'm very grateful for it. I often had to be dragged to church or church events. But I'm appreciative of the Christian values I was taught at home and in church.

Attending church regularly, being a faithful attendant, and learning to give to the church are things I'm glad I was taught while growing up. But if I'm being honest, a lot of it was done because I was told to do it. As a child in the Catholic Church, we were told when to have our First Communion and when to go through Confirmation, and our parents chose our baptism as a baby. There are reasons all these things take place when they do, and I'm in no way judging my upbringing. I only say this to point out that I didn't invest in my faith as I should have when I was younger. It wasn't until I was in college that I started

WANTING to go to church and wanted to learn more about Jesus and the Bible.

I was a member of the Fellowship of Christian Athletes (FCA) throughout high school. In FCA, I began to see what other churches were like and started building friendships with other Christians. Every Friday morning, we met in the biology classroom at the end of the hall because it was one of the few classrooms big enough to host the meeting. And since I had to be at school at 7:30 for our meeting, it also became a tradition to stop and get donuts and a Dr. Pepper. I loved walking into the tiny donut shop on Main Street with the bell over the door that would ding as you walked in and the antique cash register that would ring up my maple bar and can of Dr. Pepper. I'm not sure which I looked forward to more—my Friday morning routine of donuts and a Dr. Pepper before FCA or the meeting itself.

FCA sparked a new fire within me. Gathering with friends, starting the meeting with songs, and hearing from guest speakers who were either fellow athletes or one of our coaches was the best way to end the week. And the fact that I was willing to wake up early and be there before school began says a lot.

During my freshman year of college, when it came time to look for groups to join, I knew FCA was an obvious choice since it was a big part of my life in high school. Being part of FCA in college began to change my heart even more. I was surrounded each week by godly men and women who were all there to get closer to God, not because it checked a box. Some of them were athletes from my hometown, so I saw a new side of them. I was actually taken by surprise when I saw them reading their Bibles and listening to Christian music because that wasn't something I was used to witnessing.

Making new friends in FCA also led to invitations to attend Bible studies. Even though I had grown up in the church, this wasn't something I had ever done. And I had honestly never opened my Bible. We didn't take them to church because the verses were planned in advance and printed in a booklet found in each of the wooden pews. I was so nervous during Bible study when we were told to turn to a certain book and chapter because I didn't know where anything was. And it scared me a little. Attending Bible study was like a foreign language, and I kept waiting to be handed the cheat sheet like we were given in France.

I later realized that God was using all of this to plant seeds in my heart that would eventually spark a fire within me.

Bible studies were just one of the things which were new for me. I also began listening to Christian music and felt something stirring in my heart. I was starting to look forward to Sunday mornings and wanted to go to church instead of feeling like I had to go. Since I lived at home during college, I continued attending church in my hometown with my parents. And after I moved to Arkansas, I still drove home on the weekends to attend church with them.

As I got older, I expected to see God work in certain areas of my life. And I started getting frustrated when He didn't bring me a husband and family of my own. I was beginning to question whether He saw me and whether I had been forgotten.

At first, I still had faith that God was there but thought He just didn't care about me. And I couldn't figure out why He didn't care about me. Did I do something wrong to make Him forget about me? I didn't understand why I could see Him working in the lives of others, but I couldn't see Him working in mine. Spoiler alert. He was still working in mine, just not how I expected it or wanted it.

When my mom got sick, I still had enough faith to believe God would heal her. Even though I knew she had a serious type of cancer, I still believed she would beat it. But when that didn't happen, I became furious with God. I couldn't understand why He didn't heal her or why she got sick to begin with. My questions about being forgotten by God were starting to turn into questioning my own beliefs. I didn't see it then, but my Christian beliefs were slowly fading.

Prior to losing my mom, I was already bitter about the things He had not brought into my life. And then, the day He took my precious mother out of our lives on earth, I became angry. The kind of angry you get at someone who does you wrong, and you stop speaking to them. And that's exactly what I did. The grief of losing my mom eventually turned into me being so angry at God that I walked away from the church.

I stopped attending church, I stopped listening to Christian music, I stopped praying, and I was on the verge of no longer believing. "Did God even exist?" I started asking myself. If so, where was He when I needed Him?

As the stages of grief progressed, I spiraled down a path of depression, bad decisions, and settling for relationships that weren't good for me. Relationships that were hurting me more than they were benefiting me. Relationships that felt very one-sided with no respect from the other person. This affected my mental state more than I knew at the time, and I questioned my self-worth. I recognized I had stayed in a situation too long when I realized it was draining my joy and emotionally wearing me out. I had learned that choosing joy sometimes meant eliminating toxic people from your life. Thankfully I had a great friend who convinced me that I didn't have to engage in something that was stealing my joy.

During my counseling sessions, talking about returning to church was not a top priority for me. But once we got around to talking about it, I began taking baby steps toward trusting God again. It started with reading simple daily devotionals. Nothing pushy and nothing earth-shattering. Just a way to ease back into things.

After that, my counselor convinced me it was time for the next step of attending a church service. I already knew I wanted to try out different churches, although it's hard to describe the need for something different without offending those who raised me. But I just knew in my heart I needed more, and I owed it to myself to find out what that was.

My search for a new church began by attending different churches with various friends. I remember walking into the first service with still so much anger in my heart. It was a Saturday night service because it seemed like it would be more laid back. I didn't want to be there, but I knew I had to make an effort. They began the service with a song, and then another song, and after the third song, I began to get anxious and wondered why they were still singing. The church I grew up in started with only one song, so I was confused about what was happening. And I would later discover this is one of my favorite parts of church.

I wasn't sure exactly what I was looking for in a church, but I knew a few things I didn't want. I didn't want a small church because I felt like most of its members were probably families, and I didn't want to feel out of place by being the only single person there. Those churches also didn't have a lot of activities outside of those meant for families; therefore, I started looking at bigger churches.

During my search for something new, I kept getting drawn to one specific church. I'm not sure exactly what it was, but even after doing my due diligence and trying other churches in the area, something was still pulling me back to this one. And yes, I now know that "something" was God.

Of all the churches I attended during my search, there wasn't anything that turned me away from them. I could have joined any one and been happy. But that's not how God works. God puts people where they need to be. I didn't know until later that God was putting me exactly where I needed to be.

I began attending Sunday morning service by working it into my schedule. Meaning church worked around my life instead of my life working around my church schedule.

Although that quickly changed into planning activities around services because I began feeling that tug to WANT to be in church.

My Sunday mornings looked like this. Arrive early so that people wouldn't stare at me walking in. Sit in the back because it gives me anxiety when people are behind me. Enjoy the service and maybe take a few notes. And then leave without speaking to anyone. That's good enough, right? I was attending, so what else did I need?

Checking off the box of going to church on Sunday morning was a good start. But I would soon find out my next homework assignment from my counselor would be to find a small group.

"I think you need to find a small group to attend," she told me.

"A small group? What is that?" I asked since we didn't have those in my church when I was growing up, and I wasn't really sure what that meant.

She responded by telling me, "It's a place to meet other people and create connections with people you can do life with."

"Do life with?" I questioned.

"Yes, it would be good for you to find others who are in the same life stage as you to do things with on the weekends," she said.

"But I'm not looking for more friends," I claimed.

"Just try it," she assured me.

Whether you call it a small group, Bible study, or Sunday school, it's pretty much all the same. A place to connect with others and learn more about Jesus.

I didn't typically turn down homework assignments, so I followed through and attended a small group. It mainly consisted of other couples; therefore, I felt like I didn't fit in. When I returned to counseling the following week, I informed my counselor that I went and I didn't like it. I had checked that box, so now what? Apparently, the check on that box wasn't valid because she said I needed to go again. Gosh, I hate it when that happens.

So, I went again. And I still didn't like it. The next plan of action was to find another group to try. The good thing about a large church is that there are plenty of groups to choose from. Don't like one? Try another one. And so I did. But I found the next one was mostly couples too.

After a few weeks of pleading with my counselor not to make me attend another small group, she convinced me to try one more time. I saw in the church bulletin that one of our women's groups was starting a new study, so I thought that would be a good time to test it out. That way, I wouldn't have to join during the middle of a study. I was already going to be clueless, and being out of the loop during an existing study would have made me feel even more self-conscious.

When I walked into the women's group the first morning, I again tried to be there early so I wouldn't get the feeling of everyone staring at me.

As I walked into the room, I heard the group leader say, "You must be Melissa," which took me by surprise.

I later found out she was expecting me because I had registered for the group. Whew, I thought my reputation had preceded me.

That morning was more of an introduction to the study, but it felt like it would probably be a good fit for me. When the leader began making jokes about her morning, I could tell pretty quickly that we would get along well.

I'm happy to report that the women's group did indeed turn out to be great for me. And I was also right about the leader who became a great friend.

Making other friends in the group meant I didn't just sit in the back on Sunday mornings and immediately leave after the service. It can be hard to meet people in a large church…IF you don't get involved. The more involved I got, the more friendships I made. And once again, my counselor was right.

Small groups weren't the only thing I became involved in. I knew I wanted to volunteer somewhere in the church, but I wasn't sure what to help with, knowing I was not the type to teach a Bible study. I like entertaining kids, so I thought I might help in the nursery or preschool.

With a big church, I should have realized there were many other options. We had an event one night to learn about all the various areas to serve in. There was a breakout group for the "I don't know where I want to serve" people, so I went there. We ended a little before the other groups, so I caught the end of the discussion with the media team. No, not like the news media. Like digital media or the audio/visual team.

During service on Sunday mornings, I had already been eyeing the video cameras in the room. So, when I heard this was an opportunity for volunteering, I was very intrigued. During the informational meeting, I was given a tour of the control room. I had no idea this existed and what it takes to broadcast and record our weekly services. I was blown away and probably drooling, too, because I was totally geeking out. I'm the type who can walk around an electronics store for hours to look at techy things. So, when I saw all the equipment used behind the scenes, I was mesmerized. But I was also disappointed because I had never done anything like that and thought I wouldn't be of value. And then I heard the most wonderful words. "We'll teach you." Sold. I'm in. When can I start?

That became the beginning of my journey on the media team. I started learning roles in the control room and eventually moved to operating cameras. I wanted to learn as many positions as possible, so I could help out wherever needed. This evolved into becoming a Broadcast Director and calling the camera shots during the service. It's not exactly the type of director I dreamed of while at Disney World thirty years ago, but it's close enough!

I arrive early for sound check on a typical Sunday morning with my energy drink in hand. As the Broadcast Director, I have to know what's going to happen on stage before the service begins. Using the prepared outline, I make notes of everything I need to be aware of during the service.

Soundcheck is a time to see when the instrumental breaks take place and if there's a solo in the middle of the song. Is there an electric guitar riff at the beginning of the song? If so, I need to ensure a camera is ready to capture it.

As the lights are dimmed in the control room, and we move into production mode, I do a mic check between the camera operators and me and watch the countdown clock tick to the last seconds.

"Ok, here we go. 3, 2, 1, roll video," are my first instructions to the crew.

As the intro video plays and the worship team takes their places on stage, I direct the camera operators on which singers to capture.

"Camera 1, pick up the lead singer," I say over the communication system. "Camera 2, show me the singer on stage-left."

The video fades out, and the instruments fade in. My voice takes over the microphone between the camera operators and the rest of the crew in the control room.

"Take one," they hear as the camera switchers put Camera 1 on the screens.

"Camera 3, zoom in on the guitar and slowly pan up to his face," I continue. "Camera 4, get the choir."

As the first song ends, I see in my notes that we need to set up for the instrumental break. "Camera 5, this is the long transition, so drag it out. Standby on 5. Take 5. Great job, 5, keep it going. Camera 2, go to the lead singer. Keep going 5; we're almost there. Standby on 2. Dissolve to 2."

Once the service is over, there's a small sigh of relief as I have time to catch my breath. Directing the camera shots can be stressful, but it gives me an adrenaline rush that I strangely enjoy. It reminds me of being at the plate with two outs, bases loaded, and the tying run on second. Everybody is counting on you.

I have learned a lot about live production since the first day I stepped into the control room. But the biggest thing that has come out of my time on the media team is the reminder of how much I love photography and videography. I had always enjoyed them as a hobby but never knew how to take the skills further and turn them into a career. By volunteering at church, I was beginning to see new opportunities which could replace a job I wasn't happy in.

It's funny how God works sometimes. From becoming angry and walking away from the church, to testing out new churches, to finding a church but being a silent member, to joining a group, to volunteering, and now having an idea of my dream job.

None of these things would have been possible without one huge piece, though. In order to work on my happiness and find joy, God was also working on my heart. Faithfully attending church each Sunday was a great step, but putting God at the center of my life was what ultimately needed to happen. I had never fully done this in the past, even though I had lived by Christian values most of my life, minus the few years I questioned my beliefs. To put God at the center of my life, I knew I had to be all in. I needed to pursue a relationship with Him, but something weighed very heavy on me. My childhood church.

Being a member of a church other than the one I was raised in was a decision that not everyone would agree with. So, I knew if I was going to go all in and join a new church, then it was a step that others may not support. It was a very tough move because I knew what I wanted to do and what I thought I NEEDED to do, but one of the main people I needed to talk to about it was no longer here. I have to believe that if I could have sat down and explained it to my mom, she would have supported my decision. Maybe she wouldn't have, but that's something I won't find out on this side of heaven.

So, on that Palm Sunday, as I sat in the second row of the back section and felt like the pastor was speaking directly to me, I knew I needed to make a choice. When the choir began to sing the familiar words of "Amazing Grace", it was the sign I needed to move forward with my decision, and I believe my mom would have wanted me to love Jesus while attending a new church rather than not knowing Him at all.

When I decided to join this new church, I knew it would hurt people. And as hard as it was to know that, I also knew I had to make this decision for myself and do what was right for me. That's not to say the way I was raised wasn't right, but it no longer served me the way I needed it to. Going all in meant that I chose to be baptized in a new church. I had been baptized as a baby, but this was my way of rededicating my life to Christ, and it's why I chose to go through with it. I looked at it like a couple who has been married and decides to renew their wedding vows. They already said, "I do," but they are recommitting their promise to love each other. So that's what I did.

Deciding to get baptized and be fully devoted to a new church took a weight off my shoulders. Before making the decision, I was being pulled in two directions. I knew how I was raised and what my family wanted for me, but I also knew how this new church made me feel and what I wanted for myself. I was having an internal battle between my old church and my new church. But I knew I wasn't going to move forward as long as I was stuck in the middle.

Settling the battle inside my heart and choosing to join a new church has opened new ways for me to serve the Kingdom of God. In addition to my service on the media team, I also helped start a co-ed group for mid-life singles. It was a missing piece that several of us wanted and hoped the church would offer. There had been conversations between my friends and me, and we questioned why something for us didn't exist. My counselor challenged me to do something about it. So, I stepped outside of my comfort zone once again, approached the staff, and told them what we wanted.

"I've been talking to several friends, and we feel like there should be something for singles our age to gather together. Similar to the ministry for college-age members, but for those who are older. It's something that we feel is missing, and with a church this big, I think many others are in the same position we are," I explained.

Thankfully the staff member said, "I can help with that. What do you have in mind for the group? When do you want to meet?"

"I have some ideas, but I don't want to make decisions for everyone since the days I'm available may not work for others. I would like to see a focus group created so we can brainstorm ideas."

"That's a great idea. Let's start there," she said.

I worked with her on a plan, and then we brought in others to execute it. And now we have a thriving co-ed adult singles group that continues to gain the interest of new members each week.

Within the first few weeks of our group meeting, I heard the same things I had been feeling.

One member said, "I felt like I didn't belong anywhere because the other groups are for married people."

Another one said, "My friends are married and have kids, so I don't have people to experience life with."

And over the course of just a few months, we began building new friendships and having regular events where we socialize and connect with each other. Each time we gather, I hear something along the lines of "I'm so glad this group exists."

If you could have seen me when I heard these things, you would have seen the biggest smile on my face. And I had joy in my heart. Not because these people were hurting but because we now had a place for them to feel like they belonged and to build connections. A place to build friendships with others in the same life stage. Yes, that thing

I fought four years earlier when my counselor told me I needed people in the same life stage as me. And now we're providing a way for that to happen for one of the most missed demographics in church—single adults who are over 35.

The ability to see joy in situations has been the result of several things. And it has been God who has been working in all of it. It took a lot of work to get back to trusting Him again, and once I did, my life changed for the good. Don't get me wrong, though. There are still bad days, and there will still be challenges when bad things happen. But now I'm better equipped to make it through those times. Instead of being fearful, I trust God's plan for whatever is going on. That doesn't give me the right to be careless, but it gives me peace instead of constantly worrying.

Whether you were raised in a Christian home or not, God can work on your heart if you let Him. But be prepared to be amazed at what all He will do with your life. Who knows, He may even tell you to write a book someday.

CHAPTER 11

What started out as an hourly job after high school went from frying chicken in the deli to a more than 20-year career. Throughout my career in Information Systems (IT), I had various roles, including software development, fixing support issues while on-call, and project management. But as my time with Walmart continued, I lost my passion for it. And if I'm being honest, I never had a passion for the work I was doing. Still, I had a passion for being a team player, for making sure our team was successful, for building connections and friendships at work, for supporting myself financially, for having a job that supported my dreams of traveling, and for being dedicated to the only employer I had ever had. Those passions had sustained me enough that it didn't matter whether or not I liked the actual work I was doing. But eventually, those passions weren't enough to get me out of bed in the morning.

As the company began to change, the things I was passionate about were becoming non-existent because we no longer had the same team environment that used to keep me going. It seemed like the fun times were disappearing, and the things that made me thrive were too.

It was also a time in the company when we never knew if we would have a job the following day. We didn't know if "today" would be the day we walked in, only to be handed a severance package an hour later. It created a lot of tension and low morale, and it was stressful always to be wondering. There was constant gossip and rumors of when the next big layoff would be, creating an unhealthy environment.

Many factors played a part in the decisions I needed to make regarding my next move. Do I change roles and try to find passion in my work? Do I leave IT and find something new and exciting that will re-energize me? Or do I find a different company to work for?

And then I remembered a goal I had made seven years prior. Instead of waiting until retirement to fulfill my dream of traveling the world, I made an unrealistic goal of taking a year off from work to travel. At that time, my mom had just passed away. She was young and never made it to retirement age. It was a strong reminder that we never know when our days on earth will end. So, I told myself that I wouldn't wait until I was 65 to see the world. I told myself I wouldn't sit by and watch the years slip away, even though that's exactly what I was doing. My goal had been to take a year off when I reached 20 years with the company. I guess it was more of a joke than a goal because I never really saw myself doing it. But I was approaching 23 years with the company when it hit me. It was time. Time to take the year off. It was like the lightbulb literally came on, and I kept thinking, "That's it; that's my next move."

I evaluated my finances and knew I was prepared to make the move if I decided to go through with it. And while I knew it was what I wanted in my heart, I also knew it was a huge decision that I couldn't go back on once it was done. Could I return to the company at a later time if needed? Sure, I could. But if I was going to give up all my tenure by leaving, then going back was not something I wanted to do.

I knew in my heart that leaving was what I was supposed to do. But all of the "what ifs" kept weighing on me. What if I'm making the wrong decision? What if I don't find another job after I take a year off? What if I run out of money before I find another job? What if I can't find affordable health insurance? What if I regret my decision to leave my work family? What if I can't find what I'm genuinely passionate about, and it becomes just another J.O.B.?

Once I was 99% sure that I would go through with leaving, I began taking my unused vacation days. You're crazy if you think I was going to let those slip away! However, if I used the vacation days and, for some reason, decided not to quit, then I'd be left with no vacation days for the next eight months. It was time to get serious about my decision and commit to it. And how was I going to do that? I had to tell my dad about my plan. I had been scared to tell him, but I knew if I had the courage to tell him and get his buy-in, then it would be a solid 100% decision for me.

The day I was planning to tell him, I was nervous but excited at the same time.

"Dad, I'm thinking about retiring from Walmart," I told him.

With surprise, he said, "Are you sure? How are your finances? What are you going to do after you quit?"

I explained my financial situation to him, and he agreed that my plan was feasible.

And then I told him, "I'm planning to take a year off to travel before deciding my next move."

He knew at that moment that I truly took after him and his love for travel, so he grinned with excitement for me. He still had the same concerns I had, but he was on board with my plan.

I began planning out the dates for the remainder of my career, knowing that I had a few projects I wanted to wrap up before I left. And then, it finally came time to turn in my resignation. But only after I googled how to write one. After all, that was the only place I had ever worked, and I didn't even know what to say.

"How to quit my job?" was one search I did.

"How do I write a resignation letter?" was another.

Followed by "What to do on my first day of retirement?"

The weight was lifted off my shoulders once I turned in my resignation. I no longer had to ponder my decision because it was official. I had kept it very low-key until that point which had been stressful. Now that my manager knew, I was ready to tell others. But he still hadn't told the team, so I held off for a little longer until he could make the announcement. In the months leading up to my leaving, the manager would pull the team together in a special meeting whenever there was a promotion to announce. So, this is what I expected when I turned in my notice. But instead, he sent an email to the team. Nearly 23 years of service to the company, and all I got was an email? That was just another confirmation that it wasn't the same work environment as when my career began, and it was time for me to move on.

Taking risks is not normally in my repertoire. Not this big of a risk anyway. So even though I had made my decision, I was still shocked I was going to do it. Leave the only company I had ever worked for with no plan for my next step? "I must be crazy," I thought. But I knew God had a plan for me, and He wasn't going to reveal the next step until I took the first one.

Knowing I was risking a lot created an odd excitement within me. What I was about to do is something people may talk about doing but don't actually go through with it. And I was going to be the one to go through with it. That put a smile on my face. Not because I was doing something that others weren't. But because I was doing something for myself. I had been putting a lot of effort into being a better version of myself. Doing things for myself was not a regular occurrence, so I looked forward to doing this for me personally.

The days leading up to my last day at work were a mixed bag of emotions. At the same time, they were exciting and sad. I walked the halls through the blue and gray cubicle walls to visit my old teammates. Saying goodbye was the difficult part. Making sure the gopher had one last appearance was the fun part. And the feeling of knowing that I only had to do one more installation or one more project plan was the incredible part.

My manager asked what time I planned to leave on Friday. "Around 10:00," I replied. This gave me enough time to say my final goodbyes and turn in my laptop and badge. My manager was surprised that I didn't plan to stay all day. But by that time, I had already turned over documentation, contact information, and any leftover project items, so I'm not sure what would have been the point of me twiddling my fingers at my desk if I had stayed longer.

On Friday morning, I parked my car and began my trek through the large parking lot, and as I made my way to the crosswalk, the emotions started to hit me. I strolled down the sidewalk and turned to go into the building just as the glass doors slid open. I scanned my golden-colored badge across the entry checkpoint for the last time. I proceeded down the aisle and rounded the corner to my desk. It seemed so surreal as I took off my backpack and sat at my desk for the last time. I logged into my laptop but not to do any work. I wanted to check my email one last time. Farewell notes from my co-workers had been trickling in throughout the week as people heard the announcement of my departure. Most of the messages came from people I had worked with years ago. Again, this helped confirm the lack of team environment I had felt because the notes proved that the deepest connections during my tenure were from a time when we worked together as a team, and we felt like family.

In a way, the events of that morning had just felt like the last day before a vacation. But the moment I turned in my badge and was escorted to the door, it finally hit me that it was over. As I carried my box of personal items through the parking lot, I got emotional. Twenty-three years of dedication, and now I was moving on. A few tears managed to break through as I walked to my car for the last time. Even if there had been any doubt in my mind about what I had just done, it was too late to change it. And it was time to move on.

The tears didn't last long because the excitement took over very quickly. It was late in the morning on a Friday, and I had nowhere to be. It was such an exhilarating feeling. I was ready to start the next chapter.

A few weeks after my last day at work, I began looking at jobs. I didn't intend to apply for one, but I wanted to know what was out there and what might fit me and my passions. It was stressing me out, though, and stealing my joy of being free to wake up in the morning and not think about work. So, I made an agreement with myself that I wouldn't look at anything else until my year off was over. I had to give myself time to enjoy the opportunity I had been given. And that's exactly what I did.

Leaving my career behind took a lot of courage. It required me to step out of my comfort zone into the unknown. I didn't have a plan for what was next, so I had to trust God with the plan and rely on Him to provide for me. Provide human connections to keep me from being lonely, provide financially by making my savings be enough, provide opportunities for me to build new skills, provide patience as I waited for the next steps, and provide the next steps when it was time for me to find another job.

It wasn't until after I left my job that I realized how unhappy I had been with it and life in general. My mood immediately started changing, and I began looking forward to each day. I would wake up with ideas of how to appreciate every second of the day before it was gone. Except for the seconds before 8 AM. Those seconds didn't exist on my clock. But after I had time to sleep in, THEN I would start planning to enjoy the day.

Shortly after I quit, I noticed I began to feel like myself again. This means I started letting the real me slip away at some point due to an environment that wasn't healthy. I now enjoyed every little thing about life and found joy in so many things. Part of that is because I now had time for the things I enjoyed, which helped bring out the best in me.

I realize that not everyone can take the kind of risk I took. Being single with no kids made it less risky for me than for someone who has a family to support. But on the other hand, I could say that being single made it riskier for me because I had no other income to fall back on if I used all of my savings. So maybe taking a risk like this isn't something you can do yourself. But small changes can still be made to find joy and live every moment with intention.

Take time to evaluate the things in your life that need to change. And then be courageous enough to make the change. I didn't want to look back on my life and say, "I wish I had done______," and I don't want you to say that either!

CHAPTER 12

The family vacations we took when I was young developed into a love of travel. Traveling is a big part of me because I love to see God's creations across the country and the globe. And the travel bug runs in the family. From my Grandmother's love of camping at the National Parks to my dad's love of exploring historical sites. Whether it's seeing the mountains in the distance or the color of the ocean, I love to experience new things and be adventurous. This doesn't mean each destination has to be elaborate because I can enjoy something locally just as easy as something 18 hours away. State parks are a great way to explore without having to go very far and spend money. But National parks are at the top of my list. Unfortunately, these are further away for me. And with the limited supply of vacation days at work, it became difficult to visit places on my list while still allowing time for family over the holidays.

The year 2019 was about change, rest, and exploring. Exploring the world AND exploring my career options.

When I quit my job, my main goal was to live life and live it to its fullest potential. I wanted to see the world! I knew if I kept working the same job for another 20+ years, I'd never be able to accomplish everything I wanted to do. Generally, our bodies aren't in the best shape when we reach retirement age. And that's IF we live long enough to see retirement. My mom did not. This was my driving reason not to waste any more time and why I quit my job to travel the world.

When I sat in a cubicle every day, I felt like I was watching opportunities pass me by. Like most people, I was living for the weekend and dreading Monday mornings. But instead of continuing to complain about it and stay stuck in that same position for the next 20+ years, I decided to do something about it. I wanted more out of life, and I went for it. I knew it would require more time if I were going to LIVE life instead of just existing. And since I can't add hours to the day, I realized I had to subtract something from my day. Look at me using math outside of school!

By subtracting the thing sucking the life out of me, I re-energized my life and intentionally chose what my days would look like. I no longer had to ration my vacation days because now, every day was a vacation. Or as I liked to call it, every day was Saturday. Saturdays were always my favorite because it was the day I could sleep in and not set the alarm. It was the day that didn't have established plans. And it was the day following the last work day. This probably sounds familiar to you because I think the majority of us live this way. We are building up to Saturday all week, only to be let down the following day because we dread the next six days. I was tired of this mentality. It took me a while to figure out how to do something about it, but once I did, I didn't waste any time taking the next step.

After leaving my corporate job, the wonders of the world were at the top of my list of things to see. I know many of us have a list of places we want to see and adventures we want to go on. But mine isn't just a list to me. It's a plan. Making a list is my way of knowing how and when to schedule what's next. And having a limited number of vacation days to accomplish my plan became a roadblock. So I removed the roadblock.

I planned to travel for a year and then find a new job. Not to travel on one long 12-month journey but several short journeys where I would come home for a week or two in between. I wasn't prepared to leave everything behind for 12 months, and I knew I would get lonely if I were gone that long. And if I'm being honest, I knew there would be holidays and other events that I didn't want to miss.

After my last day of work, I began looking at my list. It was hard to decide what to check off first, but I knew if I didn't take action, I would end up sitting at home for an entire year.

I began my "retirement" with several national park trips. I even traveled internationally and added more countries to my passport. Eight months after leaving work, I went on the trip of a lifetime. It was our scheduled family vacation that my dad, my sister, and I still do together. As a family, we had been to multiple countries and continents, and it was time to check off our seventh continent.

Antarctica, here we come! It was the most fantastic trip; to date, it's my favorite.

Over the years, I have been asked regularly what my favorite vacation has been. And I've never had an answer because each trip brought something new. Some might be nature trips; some might be more about history, or possibly just a city tour. They are all different. Therefore, I've never been able to pick a favorite. Until Antarctica.

Antarctica was the place I never thought I would go to. It seemed so out of reach. I thought only explorers and scientists went there. And National Geographic photographers. How fun would it be to have that title…and their camera equipment!

While making our travel plans, we had two options to get there. We could sail from Argentina to Antarctica and then continue sailing on the same ship. Or we could fly from Chile to Antarctica and board our ship once we landed on the White Continent. If we chose the Argentina option, we would be faced with the Drake Passage, which is often considered some of the most treacherous waters for ships to cross. It's where the Atlantic Ocean and the Pacific Ocean converge, and because there are no landmasses nearby to break up the current, it creates some of the choppiest waters in the world. I know I said I like adventure, but not the kind where your bed needs a seatbelt to keep you from falling out.

Some expeditions get lucky and have smooth sailing across the Drake Passage, which the crew liked to call the Drake Lake. But you might also hear them call it the Drake Shake, and that was something I didn't want to experience.

Rather than take our chances between the Drake Lake and the Drake Shake, we chose the flying option from Chile and bypassed the voyage through the Drake Passage.

Flying into King George Island in Antarctica was very unpredictable because the weather could change at any given moment. We were given the go-ahead that morning at breakfast, so we loaded up on the buses and drove to the airport. The go-ahead wasn't an all-clear for takeoff, but it meant we were one step closer to boarding the plane.

We waited patiently in the airport, although we were sweating. We had to wear all of our layers in preparation for landing in Antarctica since there would be nowhere to change once we got there.

We wondered with every passing minute if we would get to fly that day or have to postpone.

The airport (consisting only of Antarctica passengers) erupted in excited cheers when the announcement was made that we received our window for flying.

Waiting for my seat number to board was the most anticipation I've ever had for boarding a flight!

Upon landing, when we felt the bump of the wheels touch down, the entire plane clapped and cheered in unison.

I was in awe the moment I stepped off of the plane and couldn't believe we were actually in Antarctica. As I looked around at all of the white surrounding us, it gave me a strange feeling that I can only describe as being similar to walking on the moon. Not that I've walked on the moon, and not that it's anything close to that, but that's how unbelievable it felt at that moment.

Once all the passengers were off the plane, we began our 1.25-mile trek to the water's edge. I love hiking, and 1.25 miles is short in my book. But when you are wearing rubber boots and three layers of clothes, it makes for an interesting walk.

As we walked along the path to the shore, we passed research stations and housing for the scientists who live there year-round. We were given our life jackets upon arriving at the water's edge and formed a line to board the inflatable Zodiac boats that would tender us to the ship. We saw our first penguins as we waited to board, and I raced to get my camera out and capture their picture. We were elated to see them walking around the shoreline, and looking back on it, I know the crew was laughing at us as they whispered to each other, "They have no idea what's coming!"

The Zodiac boats pulled up next to the ship, and as we entered the ship, we were required to wash and sanitize our boots. After the sanitization, we swapped our boots for the shoes we stuffed in our backpacks and stowed our boots in the lockers, which would be used every time we left the ship.

After boarding our ship, settling into our rooms, and going through the typical safety briefings, we began our overnight sail from King George Island to the continent's mainland. It didn't take long for me to realize the seas were starting to get bumpy. This was ironic since we purposely attempted to avoid the rough parts.

The safety briefing finished just in time for dinner to start. But I never made it to dinner. Even though I had taken medication for motion sickness because feeling every movement is typical for me, I was feeling the boat rock, and it wasn't pretty.

Our meeting took place right above the captain's bridge and was surrounded by a 180-degree view through the glass windows. I continued to sit for a few minutes, thinking that it would get better if I laid my head back.

When I realized the movement and the nausea weren't going away, I decided it was time to get up. I walked towards the stairs, and with every step, I began to wobble from side to side. I grabbed the handrails and slowly made my way down the flight of stairs.

I went to the room to lie down since that usually helps me. "Usually" is the keyword. I can't tell you how badly I wish my mom had been there with one of her handy butter bowls. But instead, I became best friends with the porcelain bowl that night.

While lying in bed, the urgent rush to the bathroom continued. Between kneeling on the bathroom floor and wobbling my way back to the twin-size bed next to the exterior wall of our room, I tried not to look out the balcony door at the whitecaps that were beginning to form. After disposing of my lunch at least three times, I laid back down and prayed it would stop.

The waves kept getting worse, and we still had all night to sail. It wasn't like I could yell, "Stop the car!" and make the sickness go away, and I was beginning to get a little scared. I was extremely ill with no end in sight.

My sister returned to the room with a plate of fruit the waiter had sent with her since he knew I had missed dinner.

She immediately noticed the moaning coming from my side of the room and the awkward position I was lying in as I tried to find ANY position that would feel less movement. The fruit plate looked less appetizing by the minute, and even if it interested my tastebuds, I knew exactly where it would end up in a matter of minutes.

My sister was out of suggestions and decided to call for additional motion sickness medicine. And that's when I personally met the doctor on board and got a shot in my rump. I have never been so excited for a needle to be injected into my buttocks. Within minutes I was out like a light and slept peacefully through the night.

The next morning on the way to breakfast, my sister waved at a man walking down the stairs and greeted him with a "Good Morning!" as if she knew him.

"Who was that?" I asked her.

"That's the doctor," she said with a grin.

I was so nauseous the night before that anytime I was able to open my eyes briefly, the only place I could look was the ceiling. So, when I say I "met" the doctor, I guess it wasn't a formal introduction because I never saw his face. All I remember is him asking my name and telling me to turn on my side.

We got to hop in the Zodiac boats twice a day to go on land or possibly cruise around the icebergs. The process started with going to the loading zone, where our rubber boots awaited us in our assigned lockers. After swapping our sneakers for boots, we walked through the boot sanitizing station and stepped outside onto the Zodiac. The plastic tub was filled with a sanitizing solution to ensure that our boots were clean before going on land. They want to protect the environment as much as possible and don't want the dirt, etc., from Chili to arrive in Antarctica. We even had to sanitize our boots between each stop in Antarctica to prevent things in the soil from traveling from one part of the continent to another.

On the morning of our first full day, we stepped foot on the mainland of our seventh continent. Because our plane had landed on an island the previous day, we didn't feel like it counted until the moment we touched the mainland.

We were expecting to be freezing as we walked around the areas approved by the crew, who checked for ice crevices and holes before we arrived. But to our surprise, it felt almost warm with the sun brightly shining. I wasn't even wearing my gloves. And for anyone who knows me, that's a shocker!

We later determined that our time in Antarctica was warmer than it was at home. It had snowed at home that week, resulting in 28-degree days. But in Antarctica, we were greeted with a balmy 33-35 degrees since we went during the summer months. I only remember getting cold one time when we had just finished dinner and were resting in our rooms. Over the ship's intercom, the crew announced a pod of orcas in front of the ship. So, I quickly threw on my coat and gloves, grabbed my camera, and headed to the ship's bow. After an hour of admiring the killer whales, I wished I had taken the time to put on layers under my clothes.

As we approached the shoreline with our recommended three layers of clothes, we exited the Zodiac and got the obligatory picture next to the flag that reads "The 7th Continent." I hiked to the top of the hill where a few other passengers had staked out a viewing spot. Together we sat in awe at the view surrounding us. White. White everywhere. I could have stayed there for hours. We could see the water spray from a whale blowhole in the distance. We faintly heard its clicks and whistles as it continued swimming hundreds of feet below the hill where we sat. The only other sound we could hear was silence.

When our morning time on land was over, we rode back to the ship, where we were given our re-boarding instructions. We first had to go through the boot-washing station to remove any "animal debris" from our boots and pants. It looked like a mini carwash with two rotating scrub brushes and just enough space between them for our boot. Once we were clean, we walked through the sanitizing water and placed our boots back in the locker to await the next outing.

On day two of our expedition, we docked the Zodiac boats beneath a hill known for having a penguin colony. As we began our trek up the hillside, we noticed small trenches in the snow. Not very wide and not very deep. But they were weaving around the hill and connecting to other trenches.

"Those are penguin highways," one of the expedition guides told us.

As we went further up the hill, we saw our first penguin. And then another one. And then…"Oh my gosh, there are penguins everywhere!" The tiny trenches were full of penguins waddling around. The packed snow inside the penguin highways made it easier for them to move around. But they were only wide enough for one penguin. So, we watched in anticipation when we saw a penguin coming from each direction.

"What will they do?" we wondered. "Will they turn around? Will they move over?"

We soon got our answer, as one of them stepped aside long enough for the other to pass, and then they continued along their route.

I stood and watched in amazement at their home, where we were a guest. We had been instructed to stay five meters from them, so I admired them from a safe distance and listened to their unique sound. Unfortunately, the smell coming from the penguin colonies traveled further than five meters. Penguins are cute, but they sure do stink. And if you happen to see their tail go up, you better step back because their poop shoots out like a water gun! This made me thankful for the five-meter distance rule!

I didn't want to leave the penguin colony that day because it was something I might never get to witness again. To my delight, we saw two more colonies during our expedition; each of them was even BIGGER. Thousands of penguins waddled around, building nests with rocks that they carried one-by-one to their designated spot. Momma penguins were feeding baby penguins. Penguins were molting their feathers. And penguin children chasing after their moms, who were probably yelling, "Leave me alone! Go bother your father!"

At dinner that night, an expedition crew member joined our table, which was surprising at first. Having a small ship was one of the advantages of the trip. The crew ate where we did, walked the same halls as us, and were always willing to have a conversation and answer questions.

I had just sat down with my plate of food from the buffet line when we heard a commotion on the ship's port side.

"What's going on?" we asked the waiter.

"There is a whale breaching out of the water," he told us.

We stood up, saw faces pressed against the window, and began to hear "oohs and ahhs" coming from them. I threw down my napkin and scurried to the port side as other passengers began gathering, none of us caring that our food would get cold. We each took our position as close to the window as possible, waiting for the whale to breach again.

Suddenly, the whale came out of the water and went back down with a full-body splash. I had seen whales wave their tales out of the water before, but I had never seen one breach out of the water. And it was as if he knew we were watching because he began putting on an epic show for us. For over 20 minutes, the "oohs and ahhs" got louder with every breach, and we cheered like we were at a sporting event.

It was the same excitement for each experience we had in Antarctica. Whether it was circling icebergs on the Zodiac and naming what each one looked like after seeing the ice cream cone-shaped iceberg. Or was touring the Ukrainian research station or witnessing a seal make a bed out of an iceberg just big enough for him. Or being on the water looking up at 15+ stories tall glaciers and noticing the blue crevice that penetrated the middle of it.

On the last day, after hiking to another penguin colony, there were rumors from the crew that we would finally get to…wait for it…do a polar plunge! I thought Antarctica would ultimately be the trip I didn't have to pack a swimsuit. I took one to Iceland for the Blue Lagoon and one to Australia for the Great Barrier Reef. But who would have guessed I would need one in ANTARCTICA?! I did! Because twenty-seven years earlier, I went on a white-water rafting trip that set the tone for my vacations. If it involves adventure, then I'm signing up for it!

Leading up to the polar plunge, I wondered where it would take place.

"Will we enter the water from the shoreline?" I wondered. If so, I might chicken out once my first toe entered the frigid water.

The announcement was made. "If you are participating in the polar plunge, go downstairs to the Zodiac-loading location."

I made my way downstairs with my swimsuit and robe (yeah, like that was going to keep me warm). Standing with all of the other suckers, we waited for the brave one who would go first. And once he did, the excitement in the room grew as we cheered each other on and high-fived as each person came back aboard.

Inching my way toward the front of the line, the shivers began to trickle down my body. Not from the cold, though, but from my nerves. I wasn't about to back out because I only had one chance to polar plunge in Antarctica, and I wasn't going to miss it. The nerves eventually turned into adrenaline, and it was my turn to be fitted with the safety belt. Instead of placing life jackets on each of us, the crew used a belt around our waist which was attached to a rope so they could help pull us back in.

"Oh no, it's my turn," I thought as I walked to the end of the ramp. If it had just been me on my own timeline, I don't know if I would have jumped. But I knew the crew was waiting for me, the photographer was waiting for me, the other passengers were waiting for me, and my dad on the balcony two stories above us was waiting for me.

"Go, Melissa!" I heard my dad yell.

As I stood at the end of the ramp, I looked down at the icy cold water and stared at it for what felt like several minutes. But within a matter of seconds, I convinced myself to jump.

Instantly my body was fully submerged in the 32-degree water, and I felt the shock of the cold as I flailed my arms to resurface as fast as possible.

It was over just as quickly as it started, and the crew pulled me back in. As I climbed up the ladder, another wave of shivers hit me as the wind blew across my wet swimsuit. I quickly found my robe and walked towards the other end of the room where a crew member was waiting with a tray full of tequila shots to warm us up. I gave mine away to the person behind me and then headed to the balcony to watch the remaining passengers jump in.

The thrill of waiting, jumping, and watching is something I hope never to forget. It's an adventure that may never be topped, but that won't stop me from trying to beat it.

Antarctica left me with lasting memories of an expedition of a lifetime. It was so serene and white as far as we could see. The landscapes were ever-changing because every glacier was different, and watching the wildlife was incredible.

Traveling is an example of how to live life to the fullest. It's what inspires and motivates me to be better in life. It motivates me to control my finances so I can afford to travel, and it motivates me to be healthy, so I can enjoy all of the crazy adventures when I get there. But your motivation might be something completely different, and each of us has to find what that is.

Maybe you want to spend more time with your kids. Or perhaps your motivation comes from within your job because you want to run the company someday, or heck, maybe even run your own company someday. The point is that we are all different; therefore, our goals and motivation will be different too. If I had kids, then I would spend my time differently. But traveling is my way of enjoying life despite the things I wish I had. Traveling is how I remind myself that even though I didn't get everything I dreamed of, I got so much more than I ever dreamed I'd have.

CHAPTER 13

Two months following my trip to Antarctica, I traveled to Greece in March 2020. After almost getting stuck in Athens (thanks to the U.S. travel ban from Europe) and smuggling toilet paper in my suitcase (thanks to the supply shortage in the U.S.), I finally made it back home. There I found myself on the porch, bored from playing every iPad game I could find because I had learned my last three trips of 2020 would be canceled.

"Now what?" I thought to myself.

I still had two more months off before I started looking for a new job. I had kept my promise of not looking at job openings during my year off, so when March 2020 rolled around, I still had no idea what I wanted to do next. But God did.

As I sat on my back porch during the middle of Spring Break, the answer presented itself in the form of a Facebook ad. The ad intrigued me enough to click on it, and after watching a quick video, I knew without a doubt it would be my next career move.

I immediately began taking steps to start my own Real Estate Photography business. I began learning, purchasing new equipment, researching, and thinking of a business name. A name for my soon-to-be business was probably the hardest of all the tasks on my list.

A few days later, at a meeting with my Bible study group, which had moved from virtual meetings to outside, I made the announcement as we sat underneath the 165-foot crosses at church.

"I've decided what my next step is. I'm going to start my own business doing real estate photography," I confidently told them with a grin.

I had never owned a business, but my friends had already figured out I don't just talk about doing things. I execute.

That's not to say I wasn't nervous. The thought of "selling myself" to convince real estate agents to hire me for their listing pictures made me want to curl up in a ball and eat the last of the cherry chocolate chip ice cream in the freezer.

"Who would want to hire a photographer with no portfolio to show them yet?" the voice in my head kept saying.

God's timing continued to be perfect, though. A family member gave me the opportunity to practice all of my services at their house. It was a win-win for everyone because they received free pictures, video, floor plans, and a virtual tour, and I now had a portfolio to share with potential clients.

As I began to reach out to agents, I was reminded it is something I hate to do. I had to force myself to ask others to give me a chance. I was second-guessing everything and wondering why they would choose me over another photographer. But my counseling sessions were there once again to guide me through it and give me the confidence to keep moving forward.

I was thankful to be financially stable and didn't have to "beg" people to work with me. I let the clients come to me naturally and through word-of-mouth. After all, isn't the best way to get clients through a recommendation from someone who has already worked with you?

Since I let my client list build naturally, I still had time for activities I didn't get to do while working 9-hour days. I scheduled time for early morning walks with friends, meeting new friends over coffee, afternoon bike rides, and lunch dates, where we talked for a couple of hours because neither of us had anywhere to be. I had rediscovered my childlike joy while still having the pressures of adulthood. I got to wake up in the morning and watch the sunrise from my porch. Oh, who am I kidding?! By now, you know I didn't wake up early enough the see the sunrise! But I did sit on my porch each morning and take in the stillness of the day.

As the word spread about my business and my porch time got shorter, I still couldn't believe I was successfully running my own business. Not just any business, though. I was doing what I loved and had a passion for it. I looked forward to going to "work" every day.

I would turn giddy each time I captured a picture that was portfolio-worthy. I learned to fly a drone and geeked out each time I launched it in the air. I got to see birds-eye views of the lake one day and panoramic views of hundreds of acres of land in the middle of the Natural State the next. There were times when I looked at my screen and felt like I was traveling in another country because the views were something I wouldn't see from a desk. I went from managing million-dollar IT projects to capturing pictures of multi-million-dollar homes.

When I left my long-term corporate job, one of my biggest concerns was losing the opportunity to interact with people. But God knew I needed that and provided a new career where it would still exist. I have gotten the chance to meet a lot of amazing new people who have become friends. I have networked with other business owners who have become friends. I have met leaders of local nonprofits who allow me to help spread the word about their organization. And I have met homeowners I've hired to work with me on separate projects.

I love looking back on the things that led to me finding a job I'm passionate about. My counseling journey played a huge part in it because I kept taking baby steps to determine what I wanted to do. And sometimes that meant finding out what I DIDN'T want to do. I volunteered a few times, which helped remind me what kind of tasks I didn't want to do on a daily basis. I'm not your girl if you need someone to cold-call people and ask for donations. These kinds of observations helped me know what I would be good at.

Fortunately, I knew which things weren't a good fit for me. The problem was when it took so long to figure out something that I was both skilled at and passionate about. I had been settling for things I was skilled at, but I needed more because passion is what gets me out of bed in the morning.

While volunteering at church on the media team and drooling over the equipment and free bagels on Sunday mornings, I found that passion. It opened my eyes to realize it IS possible to love what you do. Volunteering on the media team allowed me to learn new skills. Now, I just had to figure out how to get paid to use those skills. Being a full-time photographer was something I had always thought about doing, but it never seemed like it could provide a full-time income for me. But now, I had additional skills to use, and when I started my business, those skills transferred directly into the work I was doing every day. I can't help but smile when I think about how God planned that. It's encouraging to look back and see what He did, especially when I thought He had forgotten about me.

It's a journey I often look back on, especially when the future seems overwhelming. When I wonder if my singleness will ever dissolve into a relationship. Or when I question if my business can survive the ups and downs of the real estate market. And when I fear putting my words out into the world in the form of a book.

These things remind me to look back and remember how God pulled me through grief, a place I didn't think I'd escape from. When He guided me to counseling at just the right time and to just the right counselor. The first couple of years in counseling were a weekly emotional battle, but sticking with it allowed me to grow mentally, spiritually, and emotionally.

God also knew the steps I took in counseling would lead me to take risks, which eventually led to finding my dream job. Remembering these things is the only way to recognize them when they transpire. Because when you're in the moment and in the depths of grief, it seems like it will never get better. Those were the days that made it hard to choose joy. When getting out of bed was one of the day's biggest struggles, the last thing I wanted to focus on was choosing joy. I wanted to feel better instead of being depressed about all of life's challenges, but the effort I needed to have for choosing joy was spent on making it through another day. Or so it seemed.

Choosing joy is much easier than I thought it would be. I just needed a little help and guidance to get there. I needed to be reminded of the amazing things I already had in my life and that I could be happy exactly where I was.

The mindset shift of choosing joy doesn't mean I don't still have hard days.

For example, today, I saw a truck that reminded me of someone I used to know, and I still looked inside to see if it was him. I shouldn't have looked inside. Why did I look inside?! I used to let these situations get in my head. But now I'm able to handle them with ease and maybe even laugh about them. Is that my reaction every time? I wish!

I also struggle with not having a family of my own. I still have days where I want to run away to that isolated Airbnb, and those are the days when I usually end up at one of my favorite hiking spots because I have found nature to be very healing.

Does nature fix my problems? Once again, I wish! Nature does help me to cope with it, though. Being outside almost instantly takes away the heartache of the day. Instead of thinking about whatever hurt me that day, my thoughts turn into admiring the "L" shaped tree on the side of the trail, watching a squirrel dart in front of me, seeing the sun glisten on the water, and listening to the leaves rustling on trees. But if there are leaves rustling on the ground, then we have a problem. You will probably see me pick up the pace, but you won't see me look down because if there IS a snake on the ground, then I don't want to know it.

What works for me may not work for you, and that's where the work to find that "thing" comes in. Or it could be a different "thing" for each situation.

Next week is the 10th anniversary of my mom passing away, and I don't know how it will affect me because each year brings new feelings. The sadness during the first years eventually turned into remembering the good times and honoring her memory. I know there will still be sad times during the week, but I try to think of her in ways that will make me smile. Sometimes that means imagining the sound of her laugh or baking one of her favorite treats. And it might even mean an extra session with my counselor to work through the emotions. And I'm okay with that because I acknowledged a long time ago that I need people to help me through the things I'm not good at.

I'm someone who doesn't typically like to ask for help. However, I now admit I do need the guidance of others sometimes. Guidance from the ones who are trained in specific areas which I'm unfamiliar with.

Over the years, I have had the opportunity to learn from some amazing coaches because I'm not an expert in the things that I do. Therefore, I lean on the ones who are. My coaches are my saving grace. I wouldn't be where I am today if it weren't for the "coaches" in my life.

Some actually go by the name Coach. Some go by the name Personal Trainer. Some go by the name Counselor or Therapist. Some go by the name of Music Instructor. Some go by the name Teacher. Some go by the name Co-Worker. Some go by the name Mentor. Some go by the name Health Coach. Some go by the name Small Group Leader. And others go by the name Family or Friend.

As you can see, coaches come from all walks of life. And I have many of them to thank for who I am today. I would be a less-better version of myself if it weren't for these coaches in my life. And to my writing coach, who is helping me with the project you hold in your hands right now, thank you for pushing me to the finish line to get my story out. And no, you can't edit this part out.

I look at counseling this way because I needed help navigating the challenges of life. And I needed someone trained in an area I was unfamiliar with and who could walk me through the challenges. My encouragement to you is to find your coaches. Whether that's a counselor or someone else, we all need someone to guide us through the unknown.

The disappointments are always going to be there. And for me, the first step was to recognize what the disappointments were.

I may not know what it's like to fulfill the plans I made at the age of 18, but I do know what it's like to wake up each day with joy in my heart and look back on a life well-lived and that I lived with intention.

ACKNOWLEDGEMENTS

To my mom: Thank you for your unconditional love, for showing me what it means to love others, and for carrying on the family traditions that helped mold me into the person I am today. Your never-ending love was shown on a daily basis through your encouragement and involvement in everything I did. I wish you were still here to join me on the incredible adventures through the mountains and everywhere in between. And I wish you were here for one more "let me know when you get home" text. I miss you every day and look forward to the day when I'll see you again!

To my dad: Thank you for loving me and teaching me life skills and the meaning of family. I'm grateful for your support in everything I have done throughout my journey. Whether it was throwing out runners on second, graduating at the top of my class, working for a Fortune 500 company, or starting my own business, you have been there to guide me every step of the way. Thank you for being an example I could look up to in life, faith, and business. And thank you for passing down your love of travel and allowing me to explore the world with you!

To my sister: Thank you for always being willing to seek adventure with me and go on random road trips to check something off my list (and add to your list). Thank you for having my back and protecting me over the years, for taking care of me whenever I get seasick, and for graciously shielding my eyes from the zoo creatures that I don't like. Your love and support have meant a lot to me over the years, and I'm thankful we get to experience the world together!

To my family: I want to list every single one of you because you have all helped shape me in one way or another. But I would need ten more pages just for your names. So, to all of my relatives, thank you! Thank you for walking through both the good times and the hard days with me and for being there when I needed you. You have all played a part in my journey, and I'm thankful to call you family!

To my friends: If I tried to name all of you, I know I would forget someone. So, to those I have been lucky enough to call a friend from childhood until now, thank you for all the memories, all of the laughs, and all of the inside jokes. Without you, life would be boring! Each of you has been there through a different season of life, and I know God put you in that season for a specific reason, so thank you for being part of my journey!

To my counselor: Thank you for the guidance that helped me grow, and which made this new journey possible. I've lost count of all the ways I have grown since working with you. Your wisdom has inspired me to choose joy, reconnect with my faith, and take risks. Without your help, this book wouldn't have been possible because before working with you, I didn't know how to be vuner... vularb... vulnerable! Geez, words are hard! Thank you for walking me through the hard times and showing me how to celebrate the good ones!

To my trainer: Thank you for putting up with me over the years and for the weekly F.U.N. I wish I could apologize for all the times I've screamed, "I hate you," but it is what it is! I've wanted to quit so many times, but for some reason, I keep coming back for more torture. Thank you for pushing me when I need it, even if it means calling me out on social media and making me commit to running a half marathon!

To my writing coach: I still laugh about the way God placed you in my path, and I'm grateful I met you. The timing was perfect, and I couldn't have asked for a better person to walk through this process with me. Thank you for pulling the details out of me and encouraging me to be more vulnerable (there's that word again!). And thank you for the miniature counseling sessions reminding me that the emotions felt while writing a book are "normal."

To my cheerleaders: You encourage me, support me, and shout my name from the rooftop any time I begin a new endeavor. Thank you for continuously asking for updates on my latest quest and showing your enthusiasm for my crazy adventures!

To my coaches and "coaches": You taught me hard work and discipline. You taught me never to cheat during running drills; otherwise, we would be required to "hit the stairs." You taught me the skills of the game and the skills of life, like how to be a team player and how to respect your opponent. Thank you for instilling in me a good work ethic and holding me accountable.

To my church: Thank you for helping me rediscover my faith and allowing me to use my spiritual gifts to serve the Kingdom of God.

To my co-workers: Thank you for the friendships we built in the workplace and continued outside the blue walls. You made me look forward to going to work, and you became like family over the years. Thank you for welcoming me into your lives when I was new in town and supporting me in times of loss.

To my first job: You taught me the ins and outs of business and how to work with customers. I grew from an immature teenager to a responsible, successful adult. The lessons I learned while on the job have followed me into owning my own business, and I'm thankful I had the opportunity to learn the many aspects of a business.

To my Heavenly Father: This journey is a result of Your grace and unending love for me. Thank You for continuing to plant the seeds and never giving up on me. My true joy comes from knowing You. My prayer is that through the words of this book, others will see You working in their lives and they will experience the same joy because of Your great love.